fashionably LATE Real Life

Stories of (Finally!) Showing Up!

created by
DANNE ReeD

fashionably LATE: Real Life Stories of (Finally!) Showing Up!
Library of Congress Cataloging-in-Publication Date available upon request
ISBN-13: 978-0-9973823-0-3
ISBN-13: 978-0-9973823-1-0
Publisher: Danne Reed and fashionably LATE Productions, LLC

Designed by Helen Scarth, Stuf² Incorporated (www.stuf2.com)

To order this title, please visit www.dannereed.com

fashionably LATE Real Life
Stories of (Finally!) Showing Up!

created by
DANNE ReeD

Written by:

Wendy Burruel

Sherri Dahlheim

Betty Graham

Connie Grant

Tricia Guerra

Amy Machacek

Sheira MacKenzie

CJ Paulus

Linda Paulus

Danne Reed

Sherri Smith

Shirley Watson

Carla White

Connie Whitesell

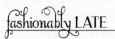

Contents

Contents

Contents

Contents

Preface

Part One: Career and Finances

Part Two: Fitness and Hobbies

Part Three: Personal Challenges

Preface

Introduction

A few years ago, through a series of life-changing events, I decided that it was finally time to make a few life-long dreams become a reality. Through the process of doing this, I realized how profoundly I had been holding myself back from living the life that I'd always wanted to live.

In truth, I had been holding myself back from being the person I always wanted to be. I simply had never had that perspective, looking at my life from the confines of the small little box I had unwittingly enclosed myself in.

Once I began to acknowledge and actively pursue what I really wanted out of life, I started noticing that I wasn't the only one who had set her dreams aside while the "business of life" commanded all her time and attention. Honestly, it's not all that uncommon. As women, we tend to be caregivers, and we easily set aside our own pursuits in order to help our loved ones achieve theirs.

That's a noble thing, and believe me, I'm not knocking it.

And yet, "go-time" comes around in every life. In every life, there is a point at which a person has to ask themselves, *"Am I fulfilling my own destiny?"*

Because I have to tell you, in my case, I learned that I was actually *hiding* behind the idea of "helping my loved ones achieve their dreams." So much so, that I was getting a little resentful toward them in my heart. My husband Craig bore the brunt of this for quite some time until I figured things out.

That's how you know, by the way, that you're not living up to your own potential. Emotions like resentment, bitterness, frustration, and annoyance with the people you truly love, are all signs that you're sabotaging your own happiness and enjoyment of life.

Here are some other signs – have you caught yourself saying or thinking any of the following:

> "I wish I would have…"
> "I always wanted to…"
> "It's too late for that now."
> "I'm too old to…"

Any one of these is a sure indication that you're holding yourself back from living your best life.

When I hear these statements, I wince. And then I get hopeful and excited.

Hopeful, because these are exactly the type of sentiments that I've seen people overcome time and time again.

Excited, because I know that when a person comes back around to believing they can achieve something that they'd almost given up on, the accomplishment is even sweeter than if they had done it when they first had the thought.

I'll tell you why this is true. When a person has a strong desire to do something – be it learning to play the piano, or becoming a real estate agent, or getting a degree – they will likely take steps to make it happen, UNLESS…

…they have a belief that they cannot or should not do it.

This "can't" or "shouldn't" belief might be a conscious one (meaning they're well aware of the reason), or subconscious (meaning the belief is somewhat hidden from them, deep in their psyche).

Some conscious "can't" or "shouldn't" beliefs might be:

- The mom who would love to go back to school, but chooses not to because she believes it would do harm to her children for her to spend time on her own pursuits.

- The working woman who would prefer to switch careers, but chooses not to because she believes that she wouldn't be able to make enough money doing what she really wants to do.

- The woman who would love to learn to fly a plane, but chooses not to because she believes she couldn't afford the lessons or the hobby once she was a licensed pilot.

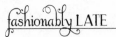

Some subconscious "can't" or "shouldn't" beliefs might be:

- The woman who loves to sing and secretly harbors dreams of inspiring people with her voice, but deep down has a belief that she's not a good enough singer.

- The woman who would love to have a healthy, loving connection with a partner, but carries subconscious beliefs about her deservingness of such a relationship.

- The woman who has struggled with being overweight her entire life, but subconsciously believes her genetic makeup will always cause her to be fat.

Whether conscious or subconscious, these beliefs, or mind viruses as the late Dr. Wayne Dyer called them, will keep us from achieving any goal or dream that we set our sights on. They do this in a number of ways:

- By keeping us from even taking the first step toward the goal ("Why should I bother; I won't succeed anyway.")

- By causing us to self-sabotage our efforts once we do take measures to achieve a goal ("I lost two pounds this week; I'm celebrating with a box of donuts.")

- By bringing up paralyzing emotions like guilt when we make progress toward our goal ("I just finished my first semester of night school, but I feel so guilty about the time I've spent away from my kids that I can't enjoy it.") As a side note, there are only two ways to eliminate guilt – stop doing what you're doing that's causing the guilt, or change your belief about what you're doing.

So, when a person finally does achieve a goal or dream that they've harbored in their mind for a long time, it means that they have at last found a way to overcome some fairly debilitating beliefs in order to make it happen. Regardless of the external challenges they faced as they were attempting to achieve a goal, the internal struggle with fears and self-doubt are often the most difficult to overcome.

It is this very thing that makes achieving a long-held dream so much sweeter.

This is the essence of achieving a dream *fashionably* LATE! Just when we think the party is over and we've missed out, we manage to beat the odds and overcome the struggles and arrive at the perfect time, making a grand entrance to the life we always dreamed of for ourselves.

Showing up *fashionably* LATE is no small feat. Unlike those who showed up early, having never doubted that they would make it to the party, showing up *fashionably* LATE requires winning internal, and often external, battles. Ultimately, it requires uprooting and eliminating an old, unhelpful self-image, and replacing it with a new one that serves us better.

Overcoming internal fears and self-doubt is a miraculous phenomenon that will affect every area of a person's life, if…they will allow it.

Why only if they'll allow it?

Because often, we achieve something amazing in one area of life without realizing that we can apply the same principles and determination to other areas. For example, someone who manages to pay off a huge amount of debt in a short time might not realize that she is equally as capable of shedding unwanted pounds using the same mindset.

It's simply a matter of being aware of what we've accomplished. We tend not to recognize or celebrate our own accomplishments. We easily see the successes of others and are amazed by what others can do, and we fail to see what we ourselves have accomplished.

Case in point, I had to convince more than one of the authors in this book that their story would inspire others. When I pointed out their accomplishment, they said, "Oh, that? I HAD to do that, and I felt like a loser the whole time I was struggling to make it happen."

And that, my friends, is the honest truth behind every success.

It doesn't feel like a success when we realize it's time to make a change. In fact, this is often a real low spot in our life. We feel like we've hit bottom and are COMPELLED to fix it.

It doesn't feel like a success while we're in what author Darrell Rosen termed the "middle miles," referring to the huge chunk of time in the middle of running a marathon where the thrill of beginning has worn off and the end is nowhere in sight. This is the part where we tend to beat ourselves up the most. ("How could I have let it get this bad?" or "I'm just going to fail again like I have in the past.")

And it often doesn't feel like a success when we've completed it. ("Well it's about time you made that happen" or "Great, that's done. Now I need to work on…")

No, it only feels like a success if we make a conscious choice to acknowledge that it was, indeed, a success.

In many ways, that is what the women who co-authored this book have done here. They are, at long last, acknowledging that what they accomplished is a great story. A story worth telling. A story that will inspire others.

From stories of learning to ride a horse to stories of speaking out loud about a traumatic event in their life to stories of shedding unwanted pounds, let these women encourage you with their persistence, their bravery and their spirit.

About this Book...

In Part I, you'll be inspired by women who made an amazing, fashionably LATE shift in their careers and financial situations. Let their stories encourage you to consider your own current career and finances and know that it's never too late to make a change, big or small.

Or perhaps you've already made such a change in your life, and you just haven't acknowledged it as a success. It's time to celebrate it, and this section will help you do that!

Have you struggled with weight loss? Do you experience frequent physical illness or discomfort? Have you harbored a desire to learn something new? If you answered yes to any of these questions, let the stories in Part II serve as motivation for you. It's true that our bodies and minds age, but consider that you could experience more energy, confidence and fun than you're allowing yourself. It's time to experience your best possible level of fun and fitness!

The stories in Part III are tales of recognizing and overcoming intense or lifetime internal battles. Do you have a hidden talent you've been ignoring, or a small voice inside that's been trying to get your attention, or a past trauma that's holding you back from experiencing life to its fullest? It's time to dig deep and discover who you truly are, and allow the real you to show up to the party of life!

Regardless of the dream, desire or goal, the real life stories in this book will entertain, encourage, motivate and inspire you to make your own personal transformation and show up for life...

fashionably LATE!

Turn the page, my friend, and let's get this party started!

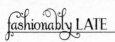

Part One

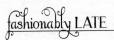

Part One

Career and Finance

"On the road to great achievement, the late bloomer will resemble a failure."

Malcolm Gladwell

The gals whose stories make up this first part of the book experienced early successes as well as failures, and at some point, realized that the path they were on wasn't quite right for them. So they made adjustments that took them outside of their comfort zone, at least temporarily, in the pursuit of a better fit, a better life for themselves and their loved ones.

In doing so, they've joined countless numbers of women who discovered their life's work later in life, and the world is a better place for it.

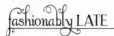

Here are just a few who have brightened our world in one way or another:

- Betty White – the actress who has made us laugh for the past few decades. What you may not know is that she didn't land a part that made her a household name until she was fifty-one (the Mary Tyler Moore show).

- Laura Ingalls Wilder – the writer whose books we know and love today didn't publish her first book – Little House in the Big Woods – until she was sixty-five.

- Toyo Shibata – a poet whom you may or may not know by name, but you'd likely recognize some of her work, started writing poetry as a spring chicken of ninety-two.

- Vera Wang – the designer of clothing and household items didn't actually design her first gown until she was forty. Incidentally, it was her own wedding gown. When she couldn't find the perfect gown, she designed her own. I love that!

- Anna Mary Robertson Moses – better known as Grandma Moses. According to legend, this artist began painting at the age of seventy-eight, when painful arthritis forced her to give up her beloved embroidery habit.

- Nola Ochs – a name you likely don't recognize, however, you may have heard about her few years back when she made national news as being the oldest person to graduate from college. She was ninety-five at the time and crossed the stage with her granddaughter who graduated with her. Apparently not quite finished with her formal education, she achieved her masters degree three years later at the age of ninety-eight.

While none of the authors in this book have reached the tender age of ninety-eight, they have each achieved a goal later in life than they thought they would.

And yet, for each of them, it was perfect timing.

We embark on our careers early in life with a set of values in mind. As we grow and learn and experience life, our values and priorities grow and change as well. For many, this feels like being trapped.

After being in a certain profession or field for a while, we settle in. We settle into the lifestyle and the routine and the income that's been developed over time.

We scare ourselves with thoughts like:

"I don't like what I'm doing much, but what if I don't like the next venture either?"

"What if I make a change and can't make enough money to support myself and my family?"

"What will my family and friends think?"

"I've got this mortgage and this car payment and tuition for my son's school…it seems selfish to risk my family's comfort for a dream."

"The field I'd like to move into is already flooded with fresh, young people who are more likely to get the job."

"I'm really good at what I do now. Do I really want to go back to being a rookie at something? How uncomfortable will that be?"

And so, we often decide just to stay put. To ride it out. To embrace what we're doing now, and ignore the small voice inside that says there's more out there for us.

After all, everyone does that. People do it all the time. The majority of people don't end up living their dream life. It's just the way it is.

Right?

Well, what if it doesn't have to be? What if you can break out of that mold and be the person who makes that major shift?

What if you're the exception to the rule who inspires others around you with your bravery and your willingness to step outside of your comfort zone to find work that fulfills you at a soul-deep level?

What if it's you who rediscovers what you're passionate about and creates your dream work life?

You're about to be introduced to a handful of women, just like yourself, who threw off "good enough" and went after "great" for themselves, and by association, their loved ones.

Each of them struggled with those same scary questions I listed above. And each of them were only able to answer those questions definitively after they had taken steps toward their goals.

You have your own doubts. Some of the questions above may have resonated with you, some perhaps did not. But if there's even the tiniest hint of a question in your mind about making a career or financial change, you owe it to yourself to check out these stories.

Let these women inspire you that it's never too late to do what you were meant to do. Your life's work is out there somewhere. Kudos to you if you discovered it early and are already fulfilled in your work.

There's a saying that's attributed to both Mark Twain and William Barclay. Regardless of which you prefer, the meaning is appropriate here:

> *"The two most important days in your life are the day you are born and the day you find out why."*

If you found out why fashionably LATE in life, join the club and turn the page for some encouragement, guidance and inspiration!

Dr. Shirley Watson is a QRA practitioner, CCN (certified clinical nutritionist), Doctor of Chiropractic specializing in nutrition and wellness, published journalist and speaker.

Dr. Shirley works extensively with the physical manifestations of ill-health, and is a firm believer that "ill health is the soul's voice wanting to be heard."

She has a three-pronged approach to reestablishing wellness in the body.

In addition to her QRA practice and the use of ERT techniques, she uses a specific and self-developed form of lifestyle coaching to help her get to the emotional, physical and spiritual drivers behind her patients' ill-health.

Chapter One

The Art of Reinvention

by Dr. Shirley Watson

"You can't stop the waves, but you can learn how to surf."

Muktananda

When other little girls my age were dreaming of lovely white bridal gowns, I was dreaming of a smart white lab coat. No one in my immediate family had an advanced education, but I knew from an early age that it was what I wanted. Though I received very little encouragement, I was myopic in my vision of being an educated woman.

The path to earning that white lab coat was long and winding and fraught with challenges, some of which I'll share with you here.

However, at the age of forty-two, I graduated from Chiropractic school, having learned many lessons along the way.

The Early Years

By the time I was nine I thought I was a grownup. My mother had a reckless calling to find another life outside our family. She disappeared periodically for a month or two, then would suddenly show up again. She would temporarily resume her tentative duties of wife and mother, only to hear the sirens' call and be pulled into the jagged shores of doom once again. As a child, I thought it was because she didn't love us enough. I realize now, sixty years later, that I will never understand her motivation. We all make choices prompted by circumstances we feel are untenable. Hers are unclear to me, and I'm at peace with that.

She died when I was twenty-seven, having had fifteen major surgeries by the time she was fifty-five, and having developed psychological challenges from enduring extraordinary physical pain and being on pain meds for years. One day we found her lifeless in her bed. Maybe her choice; maybe an accidental overdose. We'll never know.

My father was always our rock – for me, my sister – eighteen months older – and my brother – four years younger. He worked long hours to support us, and my sister and I chipped in to keep the family going, making sure there was a hot meal on the table when Dad returned from work each day at exactly 5:15. We were all making an effort to create as normal a home as possible under the abnormal circumstances. We loved each other and did the best we could.

Young Adult

While in high school my councilor encouraged me to take a beauticians' scholarship because I wasn't "college material." The only inkling I ever had that I had a brain was an English teacher who commented one day that he expected more from me based on my IQ tests -- something no one had ever discussed with me. At the time, I just figured he had it wrong.

Despite this, I never wavered in my goal of being an educated woman; it was an inner drive the likes of which blinded me from any other future. The high school councilor's comment only made me want to go to college all the more.

But I didn't understand the first thing about getting into college. A friend was attending a private Lutheran college nearby and though I wasn't Lutheran it was the only thread I could grab a hold of. I drove over to the school, figured out how to apply, got a student loan and got accepted.

And then I told my father.

He was stunned and not totally supportive. He told me that it was just a waste of time for me to get educated. That I would fall in love, get married and have kids, and it would all be for naught! He meant well, but was from an era when a women's place was with her family. His attitude only fueled my desire to forge a different future for myself than what he saw for me, and I started school in the fall.

During the first few years at college I was an awful student. I had no understanding of the effort it would take to get through, let alone shine. I was on probation my first two years. I couldn't afford to live on campus, but some new friends let me stay in their dorm room. I had to sneak in and out each day, always fearing I would be found out.

In my junior year, having worked as a waitress after classes and having saved enough money for a plane ticket and a rail pass, I dropped out of school to travel through Europe for six months. My father financed my sister so that she could go with me, and we were off on an amazing adventure, a trip that was a highlight of both our lives. We grew very close and saw the world together.

To everyone's surprise, I resumed my education when I returned, though it took me another three years to graduate. I attended graduate school, but failed to pass the tests required to get my masters.

As I had been working in the restaurant business all through school, I fell back on that once it looked like my education had faltered. Six years later, I got trained in massage therapy and opened a business doing therapeutic massage.

During this time, I became very ill – some mysterious disease that I later discovered to be Epstein Barr syndrome. I experienced extreme chronic fatigue with it, and don't really know how I survived during this time. I do know that there were friends who I thought would be there for me that never showed up, and people I never expected who showed up to help.

At Last, My White Lab Coat

While recovering from this illness, I looked into Chiropractic school. I had no money and no idea how I would accomplish it, but I called anyway. A young man answered the phone. By this time, I was thirty-eight and feeling pretty much like a failure. This young man said many things to me that day, but what stuck with me was him saying "If I can do it, you can do it."

With that bit of encouragement from a complete stranger, I began my quest to become a chiropractor.

It took another year of college before I acquired the credits I needed (I had dodged science through four years of college and two years of masters work). But finally (and at thirty-nine, one of the oldest students in the school), I attended my first day of Chiropractic school. I was asked once if I didn't think I was a bit too old to be going back to school. The truth is, it had never occurred to me, and I chose not to think so.

Financed through student loans and regular massage therapy clients, I graduated from Chiropractic school at age forty-two. I had finally learned how to be a good student. I grew to love the challenge, and graduated with honors, I'm proud to say.

And now, twenty-six years in practice, I am looking to reinvent myself again and move into another version of myself. I am an elder now and I have lots to say. In addition to writing, my mission is to help others understand that moving into a new dream, creating a new version of you is always an option as long as there is a breath left.

Still Reinventing

I have begun teaching nutrition as continuing education to Chiropractors. I've discovered that I like teaching and that I am pretty good at it. In fact, I'm having a blast doing it. Confidence is sometimes elusive, but just getting out there and facing your demons will nourish the kernel of confidence that resides deep down that will move you forward and allow you to find your voice and expand your vision.

I envision myself speaking before large groups of people, sharing my story and encouraging people to discover their most passionate self over and over again. I am also doing more writing and I am enjoying that, too. Options have always been my goal; open expression in many genres is exciting and challenging.

Lessons from a Lifetime of Reinvention

As I look back on it now, I do not feel that I had "less than" in my youth. My younger years helped forge the independent version of myself that ultimately emerged. I trust the path that my life has taken, and feel blessed for every opportunity to become that better version of me. Though, like all of us, I have moments of sadness and self-doubt, I feel outrageously blessed and optimistic about life, and am filled with adventure and joy.

I forged my way forward in my life by finding teachers and mentors whose message resonated with me. A chemistry professor in college was one of many amazing, compassionate, and supportive people I would meet along the way. Jack Canfield was an early mentor; Bruce Lipton taught me a new way to look at science; Candace Pert was a brave new voice in science when women were viewed as less intelligent than men; Muktananda, whom I met in the eighties gave me the most precious gift of all – meditation.

From each of their messages, I took what worked for me and built my own working philosophy that to this day continues to be dynamic and expanding. I am grateful for all these people and many more who provided a model to which I could aspire and articulated their knowledge in a way that I could hear it when I was ready to listen. My faith tells me that we are all part of a greater whole that guides us and lets us know whether we're on-track or not. Through meditation, I listen closely every day and am guided to be my best self.

I've learned that each of us are many people in a single lifetime, expressing a myriad of passions, experiencing many failures and many triumphs. Often it is our perceived failures that manifest as the stepping stones on which we balance to reach our next triumph.

Life is such an amazing journey and I have come to truly realize that what we focus on creates our life. I choose to focus on the wonder and the joy and the ever-expanding opportunities that are there for me, for all of us.

Dr. Shirley's Tips for Arriving fashionably LATE for:
Reinventing Yourself

ॐ Keep an open mind. "The times they are a-changing" is a euphemism as relevant today as it was yesterday and will be tomorrow.

ॐ Choose not to think that you're too old for anything.

ॐ Remember that what we perceive as failures often become the stepping stones on which we balance to reach our next triumph.

ॐ Discover mentors whose message resonates with you and learn from them.

ॐ Your life is created by what you focus on, so focus on the joy and wonder.

Dr. Shirley Watson

Sherri Dahlheim is a successful Health Coach and graduate of the Institute for Integrative Nutrition®. Her motto is *"All things in moderation."* Drawing on her extensive, cutting-edge knowledge in holistic nutrition, health coaching, and prevention, Sherri helps people make lifestyle changes and choose health-promoting ways. She co-creates personalized actions based on her clients' goals, to move them toward their ideal vision of health within their unique body, lifestyle, preferences, and resources.

Sherri happily lives in the Atlanta, Georgia area with her husband athlete and holistically healthy daughter. Information on her Health Coaching practice can be found at *HealthCoachSherri.com*

Chapter Two

Take The Leap!

by Sherri Dahlheim

"Sometimes your only available transportation is a leap of faith."

Margaret Shepherd

Do you have a desire or passion that you've wanted to do, but just haven't gotten around to doing it? I certainly did. I toyed with the idea of becoming a Health Coach for over five years before taking the leap to pursue my certification.

The interest

For most of my adult life, I read the theories and practical advice of the pioneers and experts in Functional and Alternative Medicine.

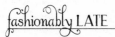

I subscribed to a Community Supported Agriculture program that provided me and my family with fresh, locally-grown produce each week.

This produce, often varieties and choices that I wouldn't normally have picked up at the market, became the catalyst for weekly research, menu creation and, eventually, a blog that I started so I could store and share recipes on how to turn the fruits and vegetables into something that my husband and I could enjoy, and my young daughter would actually eat. From that experience, we decided to dabble in subsistence farming in our backyard.

Growing our own food and creating my own recipes was so much fun, not to mention the many other health benefits it provided. I began to daydream about how much I would love to help other families experience the joy of eating healthy.

The Research

But there was a problem. The study of nutrition and strict diets didn't interest me, so becoming a dietitian or nutritionist sounded to me like drudgery, rather than joy. I was simply interested in helping people make healthy food choices, and showing them how that could fit in with their busy family lifestyle.

Inspiration struck when a friend introduced me to the concept of Health Coaching. I researched opportunities for certification and found the Institute for Integrative Nutrition® Health Coaching Program, which appeared to be the perfect fit for me. I could attain my certification in a year. I would learn the most popular dietary theories. And the best part was that all of my favorite alternative medicine experts were guest lecturers in the program!

What could possibly stop me?

You might be thinking at this point that I dropped everything and enrolled in the program right away.

You would be wrong.

Not only did I not enroll immediately, but it would be more than four years later before I finally signed up.

Like many of us when faced with a big, potentially life-changing decision, I hesitated.

For a really…long…time.

There were so many reasons for my "hesitation" – not enough time, not enough money, the "wrong time" in my life. After all, I was a full-time Mom working part-time outside the home.

Within a couple of years, I was a full-time Mom working full-time outside the home. In fact, it never seemed to be the "right time" and my income was never enough to cover the cost of the program. I was working in a job that did not suit me at all. The person I worked for was dishonest, demanding and manipulative.

Headaches were a daily occurrence for me.

I felt defeated and depressed. My relationships were suffering. I was suffering.

I knew I had to make a change.

The Leap

It all came to a head one day when my boss called me into his office and announced that I would no longer be paid for the fifty hours a week I was working, but would only be paid commission on sales.

And that was it. That was the catalyst that sparked the change.

I quit my job and, with the help of my sister, was able to maintain a small income while I evaluated my next steps. My sister was in the process of following her own dreams and I felt inspired to do the same. I realized that the desire to become a Health Coach had never gone away; it was still there waiting for me to find the time and money to make it happen.

I started another full time job that better fit my spirit and desire to help others. I worked there two years before I found the opportunity that would allow me to join the program. Finally, I was making enough money to cover the cost of the course and I had the flexibility to schedule time for my coursework.

Excited about the possibilities, I took the leap and enrolled in the course.

On the Path

The journey was challenging. I was still a full-time Mom and a full-time employee. I added part-time student to my list of titles. In order to keep up with my studies, I scheduled short periods of time through the weekdays for the modules and assignments and blocked out longer chunks of time on the weekends to catch up when needed. I had a desire to learn and was passionate about the subject, so I made my studies a priority.

There were trade-offs, of course. Household remodeling projects were put on hold so that we could make the financial investment in my studies. I gave up my favorite TV shows and instead watched my training videos. I sometimes had to sacrifice time with my spouse and family, knowing that my coaching business would later afford me the flexibility to spend more time with my loved ones.

Halfway through the program, I became plagued with doubt. Questions swirled through my mind – Did I know enough to be a Health Coach? Did I have what it takes to be successful? Was I ready to launch my business? I was determined to answer "Yes!" to all of those questions. With the help of my support team (my husband, daughter, sister, and accountability coach), I was encouraged and aided through the program. I hunkered down and refocused.

Sweet Success

The coaching program was better than I ever expected. I learned from my heroes in the health industry. I tried foods and dietary theories that I didn't know existed. I was reminded that we are spiritual beings in a material world and health isn't only about the food we eat. I became a healthier person in all aspects of my life. I made friends with my classmates and found an accountability coach that continues to support me in my personal goals. I started a successful Health Coaching practice to encourage others in their journey of health for themselves and their families.

I am now able to inspire others to take their own leap to a better life. It feels amazing to know that I can be an example as well as a support to others that need it.

What I Learned

Through this process, which really began years ago with a tiny seed of a thought, I realized that I truly did have what it takes

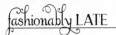

to make my dream a reality. I conquered my doubts, fears and challenges before and after signing up for the program. I devoted much time to my studies, completed the program and am now a successful Health Coach.

One key to my success in the program was my support team. The encouragement from my sister helped me to foster the dream. The assistance from my husband in taking over most of the household and parenting duties afforded me the time to devote to my studies. The cheerleading from my accountability coach, and the ongoing pledge of personal improvement motivated me to grow week after week.

I learned to move past my doubts and insecurities and take action. The actions were small at times, but each one brought me closer to my goal of becoming a successful Health Coach.

Advice

If you have a passion or interest or desire that you've wanted to pursue, you won't regret finding a way to make it happen. You may have to take baby steps, but take them, no matter how small. Move in the direction of your desired goal. Figure out what needs to be done to overcome the obstacles.

If finances are an obstacle, take an honest look at what you're spending your money on and cut out unnecessary spending. There are so many resources available to help you with budgeting. Research ways to finance your dream, or ask about payment plans.

If your obstacle is time, track how you spend your time and prioritize activities that will bring you closer to your goal. That may mean that you temporarily give up time spent on things you enjoy now in order to have more time to enjoy them later.

Most importantly, build your support team. It may be a spouse, a sibling, a friend or a teacher. Find people that will encourage, inspire and assist you in your journey, and be around them as much as possible. Celebrate and support them in their goals as much as they support you.

And then, simply take the leap!

My own leap into following my passion has changed my life for the better in too many ways to list – from how I feel about myself, to my relationships with family and friends, to my financial prospects, to my ability to inspire others to enhance their own health and the health of their loved ones.

Take your own brave leap into whatever you're passionate about, and be ready to be amazed by the transformation you inspire in yourself, as well as everyone around you.

Sherri's Tips for Arriving *fashionably* LATE to:

Following Your Passion

- Taking a leap into something often requires baby steps in the beginning.

- Be honest with yourself about where you're spending your time and money. Then choose wisely based on what you really want for your life.

- Develop a support group. You're good on your own; you're great with a team.

- Expect challenges to come up as you're pursuing your goal. It may not be smooth-sailing throughout the entire process, so plan to rely on your support group to help you through the rough patches.

- Know deep-down that you were meant to pursue your passions, and that you are fully capable of achieving whatever it is you desire for your life.

Sherri Dahlheim

⟡Through life's challenges, big and small, Linda Paulus has refined her talent for bouncing back and becoming stronger than before.

In her recovery from two major financial setbacks, she realized and now fully appreciates that it's the simpler things in life that bring the greatest joy.

For her, this means spending time with loved ones, especially her grandchildren.

Linda's story is a shining example for women struggling to recover financially and emotionally after a life-changing event, demonstrating that a fresh start is not only possible, but within reach.

One simply has to search within to find those guiding principles.

Chapter Three

A Glamorous Life

by Linda Paulus

"When we feel stuck, going nowhere – even starting to slip backward – we may actually be backing up to get a running start."

Dan Millman

As my fiftieth birthday came and went, I was hundreds of miles from family and friends, going through a second divorce, and in debt to the tune of $60,000. Not exactly living the dream. And certainly not anywhere near how I envisioned my life would be at my half-century mark.

As bad as I felt going through yet another divorce, the most daunting and overwhelming part of considering my future was the weight of all that debt. I remember feeling as if I would never be able to pay it all off, and that I wouldn't be able to support myself while paying off the debt, too. This was especially painful, because prior to both of my marriages, I had NO credit card debt. Zilch, zero, nada.

I was raised by parents who lived by the philosophy that if you didn't have the cash to pay for it, you hadn't earned it yet, and therefore you didn't buy it. Unfortunately, I didn't marry men with the same financial values.

In both divorces, I walked away with an enormous amount of debt. In my first divorce, I paid off $8,000 before the divorce was even final…in nine months' time. I went into my second marriage, once again debt-free, and came out of it with the $60,000 in debt that I mentioned previously.

During proceedings of my second divorce, I again willingly took responsibility for every single credit card balance that had my name on it, regardless of who made the actual purchases, and regardless of who got to keep the items that were bought on the card. I knew how my ex did NOT pay his bills. There was no way I would allow him to control my future financial security the way I allowed him to control me throughout our eight-year marriage.

So there I was, starting over again. Packing up my belongings, moving back to St. Louis where I grew up, and calling my Dad to ask if I could move in with him until I got back on my feet.

Of course, he said yes.

And while I was so grateful, I'll admit to feeling like a complete failure for having to do it.

As I got reacquainted with friends I had lost touch with since I moved away, it was downright humiliating to tell them that I had moved back in with my Dad because I couldn't afford my own place.

After a full year of living with my Dad, a house that I owned (the house that I'd raised my babies in) became available. The woman I had been leasing it to for years decided not to purchase it and moved out. So I packed up my belongings again and moved into this one-hundred-year-old, five-bedroom, two-bathroom, eighteen-hundred-square-foot fixer-upper with "so much potential."

In order to be able to cover the monthly mortgage on my salary, I went for a whole year with no television reception. Cable TV was a luxury I couldn't afford. I watched a lot of movies that I already owned and rediscovered the beauty in borrowing DVDs from the local library. I didn't buy new clothes. I didn't eat out. I didn't travel. My iPhone and Facebook® profile were my social life, my only regular links to friends and the world.

Yet, the old house was still more than I could keep up with. It was a handyman's paradise, but it was nickel-and-diming me to death. The pilot light on the heating system kept going out, and I had no funds available to replace the twenty-year old unit. Windows needed replaced; electrical systems needed updating.

One March day, the dam broke, literally and figuratively. I came home from work to find that a lovely waterfall had developed in my hallway. Further investigation revealed that the "Forest Lane Falls" extended into the bathroom, my master bedroom and master closet.

I'm not kidding, the sight of the disaster was so shocking and thorough, I could have sold tickets.

Didn't think of that at the time.

As it turned out, an upstairs bathroom pipe had burst not long after I had left for work that morning, and had been pouring through my home and belongings for hours.

That…was my meltdown moment.

All of the pressures and the strain and the stress and the hurt of the past couple of years washed over me. Frustration, anger, resentment and sadness poured out of me like water from busted pipes. I sank to the wet floor, my head in my hands, and cried the tears of a woman who had hit rock bottom.

How could this be happening to me?
How could this be my life?
What was I doing wrong?
Where had I gotten so off track?
When had things gone south?
Why hadn't I fixed it?
Why had I let my life get this bad?

My private "pity party" lasted about twenty minutes.

Then I got up and called the insurance company, who eventually gave me a check for the repairs. I called trusted friends who provided much-needed sympathy and greater-needed pep talks. I called the mortgage company and within weeks completed a short sale on the home. I moved into a two-bedroom, third-floor walk-up apartment with no washer/dryer hookup.

Getting out from under the crushing mortgage provided much-needed wiggle room in my monthly budget. It hasn't been all smooth sailing – I lug my laundry down and up three flights of outdoor stairs once a week, and my car has been backed into twice in the two years I've been in the apartment. But the silver lining from these little misfortunes, including the indoor waterfall disaster, is that the insurance money was a huge financial help and the lack of washer/dryer hookups allows me to spend one evening a week visiting my Dad while doing my laundry at his place.

In addition to living simply and paying down debt with all available financial windfalls like insurance payouts and annual tax returns, my strategy has been pretty straightforward. I paid off the smallest credit card balance first. Then I doubled down and paid off the next smallest balance. And then the next. And the next. You get the idea.

During this time, I was also paying off my oldest daughter's student loans, as well as a personal loan borrowed from my parents while I was married.

So here I am, five years later. Five years since I began anew – financially, emotionally, geographically.

And I'll just say it – the struggle to rebuild financially has been… less than glamorous.

And yet…I am now – one hundred percent – free from credit card debt. My daughter's student loans have been paid in full. I'm still working on the personal loan from my Dad, and I worry a little that I've missed something, that some debt I've forgotten about will come sneaking up on me and catch me unaware. So I'm not completely there yet. But I'm oh, so close! In fact, by the time this book goes to print, I'll be completely debt free.

Over the past five years, I've had time to think about what all of this means for me. Yes, I no longer feel like a slave to credit card companies. Yes, I'm enjoying the freedom of that immensely. And yes, I can now enjoy life more -- spending a little here and there on myself, my children and my grandchildren, with the knowledge that the money I spend has already been earned and it doesn't come with a hidden finance fee.

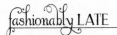

But the diamond in this story, the beautiful, sparkling, unbreakable and precious gem of truth for me is that with every payment I made, I felt like I bought back a little of my dignity, my pride, my self-confidence…until all three are now fully mine again.

And that…is the foundation of a VERY glamorous life!

Linda's Tips for Showing Up *fashionably* LATE for:

Being Debt-Free!

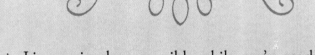

- Live as simply as possible while you're working on debt reduction. You never know, you might find it enjoyable and less stressful.

- It helps, mentally and emotionally, to pay off your smallest debt first, then applying that same payment amount to the next smallest balance, and so on.

- Make a list of inexpensive activities that you love to do, like going for a walk or taking a bath, and celebrate your small financial successes often by enjoying one of them.

- Look for the silver lining in all situations. You never know what can come from something that appears a disaster.

- Keep your chin up. Consciously spending less can feel like drudgery at times, but the end result – being out of debt – is well worth the effort.

    Betty Graham is the President of Frisco Lender Services, LLC (FLS), an appraisal management company and provider of flood certifications and IRS tax transcripts to mortgage companies. With over 19 years of sales, management and operations experience in the mortgage industry, Betty grew the company from two to over 60 employees, producing over 85,000 appraisals per year. Through Betty's leadership, the organization is known for having a culture of pride, professionalism and extraordinary customer service. Betty holds a B.S.B.A with a minor in Management from Indiana Wesleyan University. She is a current member of the Collateral Risk Network Association and the National Mortgage Bankers Association.

Chapter Four

The Secret to Success

by Betty Graham

"When life puts you in tough situations,
Don't say 'Why me?',
Just say 'Try me!'."

InspirationBoost.com

How did I get here? How did this hard-headed teenager go from conquering the world to a complete mess by the age of twenty-three? I was so angry with myself, with the world, but mostly with God. Why would He allow this to happen to me?

I worked so hard to make something of myself and yet every turn I made was just another disaster.

Wasn't He supposed to take care of me? Wasn't He supposed to show me the way?

I thought, if that was the case, why was this so difficult?

A Rough Start

You see, by the age of twenty-three, I had quit high school at the end of my junior year, and was living in a trailer park while working three jobs – one full-time job and two part-time. My marriage was in complete shambles and, if that wasn't bad enough, I had brought an innocent baby girl into this world of complete chaos and dismay.

Needless to say, I was terrified. What was I going to do? I was barely able to take care of myself; how in the heck was I going to provide for this child? It wasn't fair to her. This wasn't how my life was supposed to be.

Boy, was I feeling sorry for myself!

Looking back, I realize it was that beautiful girl who gave me the courage to take the first steps toward a better life. I left my volatile marriage, took a promotion at work so I could quit my two part-time jobs, and spent the next year trying to bring some form of normalcy back into our new lives.

Building Momentum

As time passed, I could finally start to see light at the end of the tunnel. Don't get me wrong there were several more years of two steps forward, one step back. Some good decisions, some bad decisions.

By my mid-twenties, I was working as a temporary employee for a local mortgage company. I didn't have any office experience, so the only position I could be considered for was an entry-level admin.

Sometimes you have to take what you can get, right?

Making eight dollars an hour was barely going to pay the bills, but I thought if I could get my foot in the door, I could prove myself and possibly be offered a higher-paid position.

Luckily, that is exactly what happened.

I spent the next several years doing anything and everything asked of me. I pushed for every opportunity I could get. Over the span of ten years, I worked my way up through the ranks and eventually into underwriting.

I was asked to lead the start-up of a new product mix and then start up a new division. Eventually, I worked into a sales position. I was loving life.

Although I still wasn't financially where I wanted to be, I just kept thinking if I really focused and built my client base over the next couple of years I could be killing it.

To be honest, at this point it didn't take much for me to feel like I was killing it. Regardless, it was still more money than I had ever made.

About six months into this great sales role, our company was bought by a larger mortgage company. To say I was scared would be an understatement, but I was fortunate enough to maintain a sales position with the new company.

Early on, my sales flourished. I was making more money than I had ever dreamed of making. About a year in, I was promoted to a sales manager.

For the first time in my life, I felt like all my sacrifices and hard work had finally paid off. Finally, we weren't living paycheck-to-paycheck; we were living large! I was traveling and having all kinds of fun spending all this newfound wealth.

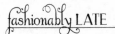

And then it happened – the call that would once again turn my world upside down.

That Monday morning started off like every other. I crawled out of bed, stumbled over to grab my coffee and sat down to emails. An hour later, I received an email mandating that all employees be on an 8:15 conference call.

Instantly, I got that pit in my stomach.

You know the one I'm talking about – the one that tells you something bad is about to happen. I just knew this wasn't going to be good.

Sure enough, that call changed my life forever.

All of our banks had called our margins due. We were bankrupt. By Wednesday, I was unemployed, along with several thousand others.

I won't lie and say I wasn't worried. But I also knew I had never had difficulty finding a job. I got busy trying to locate a new position in the mortgage industry. Week after week went by with no success.

Not only was I not having success, but the industry was completely imploding. Lending institutions of all sizes were going bankrupt…hence, the mortgage meltdown that crippled the U.S. economy in 2008.

Month after month passed, and I started to panic. I kept thinking that even though I didn't have a degree, my experience and work history should at least get me an interview.

I knew if I could get an interview, I could sell myself. I couldn't even get that far. It was crazy. I couldn't imagine what I was going to do.

In an effort to keep my sanity through the ordeal, I walked every day.

I never walked so much in my life.

Day after day, my husband went to work, and I went for my daily "woe is me" walk. You know, the God-why-me, I-don't-deserve-this, I've-worked-so-hard, why-is-this-happening, why-can't-I-ever-get-ahead walk. Whaa…whaa…whaa!

A Fresh Perspective

Then one morning, about a mile into my walk, a thought hit me like a ton of bricks. Once again, I'm allowing myself to be a victim.

And more thoughts…Really, am I going to do this? Fall victim to circumstance? Are you kidding me?

And then, another pivotal moment in my life. I realized it was time to quit feeling sorry for myself and take control of my life. I was faced with a decision – to be a victim or a victor. I turned and went straight home, picked up the phone and started calling colleges.

I enrolled in college and started a new job. Although the income was about a third of what I had been making, it was enough to pay the bills while I worked on my degree.

I also made a commitment to myself to focus on my blessings. I began every day by saying what I was thankful for and acknowledging all the good going on in my life.

A year into school, one of the executives from my old company invited me to lunch to discuss an opportunity with a mortgage company he just went to work for. He offered me a position managing a new process. It was nothing elaborate but it was a pay increase, and I loved the industry.

I took the job.

Within a few months, the owner decided to take the process I was managing and start a separate company. I was asked to build it and run it for them. And that's exactly what I did.

We spent the next eight months putting the company together, and by April of the following year, we were official.

The next three years were a whirlwind, building the business while finishing my degree. There were many long days and much hard work. But it ultimately paid off.

I'm proud to say I graduated Magna Cum Laude and was promoted to the President of the company.

The Secret Revealed

Looking back, I realize two things. One, my anger was misguided. And two, I lacked faith.

The truth is we typically don't understand the reason for the difficult lessons in life, but they are just that, lessons.

Each of us encounters trials in our life, some more than others. I believe those trials present themselves so we are able to grow and become better versions of ourselves.

I'm grateful for every tear shed, every scary moment, every disappointment, and every failure. Without them, I wouldn't be who or where I am today. It was the hard times that pushed me to go beyond my comfort zone, to reach out and take a leap of faith in hopes for a better life.

You know the saying, "if I can do it, anyone can do it." This couldn't be more true. We think we have to have all the answers, the perfect skill set, or a college degree. That simply isn't true.

I'll tell you what is true. The true secret to success.

It's YOU.

YOU are the secret to your success.

You, with a burning desire to be the very best possible version of YOU.

You, with the confidence and belief that you have the ability to be ANYTHING you want to be.

You, with the utmost trust in yourself to know, no matter what comes your way, you will make the best of it.

There are no limits if you don't allow them.

Trust me, I know it can be scary and I still have those feelings myself, but don't be afraid to take the chance and do it anyway.

Betty's Tips for Showing Up fashionably LATE to:
Success

- Ꙩ Remember that life's challenges are there to help you grow and become a better version of yourself.

- Ꙩ In any circumstance, you have the power to choose to be a victim or a victor. Choose in favor of your best, most powerful self.

- Ꙩ Be grateful for the disappointments and failures in your life. Without them, you wouldn't be the amazing person you are today.

- Ꙩ If you've been telling yourself you need something else – the answers, the perfect skillset, the degree – before you can be successful, let it go. The only limits are the ones you allow.

- Ꙩ Trust yourself. You'll make the most of whatever comes your way.

Sheira MacKenzie coaches mortgage professionals on how to build a six-figure+ business and life with balance.

In addition, she is passionate about sharing healthy aging solutions with those who are looking to end the dieting rollercoaster – once and for all.

As a mobile entrepreneur, she relocated to Charleston, South Carolina, where she is beginning a whole new chapter – new city, new community, new connections, and a whole new life!

Her purpose is clear: "To use her experience and expertise to inspire and teach others to joyfully reach their highest potential!" You can connect with Sheira at *connectingyourlife.com*.

Chapter Five

Dream Life Through Purpose

by Sheira MacKenzie

"Have the courage to follow your heart and intuition.
They somehow already know what you truly want to become.
Everything else is secondary."

Steve Jobs

Have you ever wondered if it's possible to create the life of your dreams? At the age of forty-one, I picked up a book that claimed to hold the answer to that very question. Through this book, I was introduced to ideas and principles that, consistently applied, the author wrote, would practically guarantee such a life.

Eight years later, I finally believed it. So I did what I felt called to do – I took a giant leap of faith and never looked back.

Growing up as the daughter of missionaries was both a blessing and a curse. A blessing, because I couldn't have asked for better parents. My dad was a maverick – an entrepreneur of sorts, with a heart for service and a spirit for adventure. My mother was, and still is, pure joy. She has the ability to see the best in people, and that gift allows her to be present with anyone in the room. Every person that comes into contact with her is a better person for it. I am blessed to have the best parts of both of them…along with some not-so-great parts that God decided were necessary for me to fulfill my purpose and serve others.

And it was a curse, partially because we moved so many times, and partially because my friends tended to be from wealthy families. Surrounded by so much affluence, I ached for all the material wealth they had.

However, my parents followed their calling and found fulfillment in their work – money was certainly not the center of it. At a young age I decided that following your heart meant "just getting by" financially. Following your heart meant that you may be happy, but you certainly would not be materially rich. So when I got older, I was determined to succeed financially. Thus, my quest for money began.

During college, I waited tables at busy cocktail lounges, then began a career in sales that would lead me to various industries including cell phones, telemarketing, payroll, legal services, printing, and finally mortgage lending.

For a long time, I seemed to excel at whatever I did. I had an entrepreneurial spirit, a gift for sales, and an innate ability to connect with others.

Regrettably, I also managed to forge an intimate relationship with alcohol.

Between the ages of eighteen and thirty-eight, this became the most important relationship in my life. What began as casual and social, quickly escalated and then became my standard method of self-sabotage as soon as I would reach a certain level of success in my life.

As my life took a very ugly turn, prayer became my refuge, until finally, on December 15, 2003, I asked Him to grant me the will to quit. On this fateful day, I surrendered my alcoholism and sought help. The work I did in Alcoholics Anonymous that first year was my introduction to personal development, and the key that would unlock my dream life.

Invest in You

Through sobriety and a twelve-step program, I began to understand that only I was responsible for the life I had created. No one was to blame. It wasn't fair, but these were the cards I was dealt, and this was how I chose to play them. I learned to work with what I had, with the reality of my situation at that time.

Two years into my mortgage career, I began listening to leaders in the industry who introduced me to mentors like Brian Tracy, Zig Ziglar, Tony Robbins, and Jim Rohn. I became a voracious reader. I devoured personal development books, such as Jack Canfield's book *The Success Principles* (of which I was smitten by the content), and listened to CDs in my car as I drove to appointments.

We all have blind spots that prevent us from being our most vibrant, successful selves. Once I committed to ongoing "inner work" I became open to knowing what I didn't know. I started to truly fall in love with myself and began approaching my life in a different way.

In 2010, I created my first vision board – a visual collage of dreams and goals – with pictures of waterfront homes, Eva Mendes on the cover of Shape Magazine (I was thirty lbs heavier at the time), our company Scorecard listing me at No. 3 with loan revenue of $50 million (I was doing $7 million that year and was probably in the lower third of our national sales team of six hundred), and four $100,000 bills that were placed diagonally on top of one another. I saw this board every day as I got dressed and began to "see" myself as a Top Producer.

I began to believe that those things were possible, even though the day-to-day changes were minimal.

Three years later, I was ranked No. 3 in the company and ended the year with $59 million in sales. We closed on a waterfront home in Portsmouth, Rhode Island, that mirrored the photos on my board – right down to the multiple decks on the back. My income for the year was $465,000. And within months, I would be introduced to the lifestyle solution that transformed my weight. I was at the top of my game!

Save, Regardless of the Day

In my "previous life" I had not been responsible with my money. Growing up, we had what we needed. As an adult, it took me a while to learn how to responsibly manage "more than enough." So when I was building my mortgage practice, I committed to maxing out my retirement plan and saved up to sixteen percent of my income each year.

This habit came in handy when, at forty-nine years old, I grew restless.

Taking a cue from my personal development learning, I began my quest for my next adventure by first assessing what I loved to do, which was speaking, leading and inspiring people. I knew I had a story to tell and a message to share.

A friend introduced me to a company that had changed my life and lit me up like a Christmas tree, which was a level of excitement I hadn't experienced about my work for a long time. With that entrepreneurial gene I had inherited from my father, I began to entertain thoughts of taking my career in a whole new direction.

I looked at my retirement account and realized that I had saved enough to cover my overhead for more than a year. This meant that I could follow my heart, without immediate financial pressure. I had a heartfelt conversation with my husband about what I knew I was being called to do.

And then I walked away from the successful, predictable business that I had built over the past twelve years.

I leapt in faith!

Find Your Tribe

As my personal development journey evolved, so did my relationships. I had embraced the concept that we truly are the average of the five people we spend the most time with. Slowly, I began to let go of some of the toxic, negative people in my life to make room for people who were ready to support my growth - both as a person and in business.

I also prayed that God would bring women into my life that shared my faith...that I could grow with spiritually and professionally.

What we focus on expands, so when I took the leap to go out on my own it was critical to surround myself with other entrepreneurs and people who were also committed to personal development. I was drawn to those with a mission to make their mark on the world - to seek impact, not just accumulate wealth.

Most of these relationships are virtual, and I am forever grateful to social media for keeping us all connected.

We are not meant to go through life alone, and when you are in transition - personally or professionally - a mastermind group of like-minded people committed to each other's success can be a lifeline.

Honor the Process That is Your Life. And Don't Compare Your Beginning to Someone Else's Middle

It took me two years to hone my strengths, to determine where they are best used, and to discover whom I am meant to serve. It has been challenging, and more than a little uncomfortable. There were periods when I completely shut down, physically, mentally and emotionally.

I was naive enough to think that I would embark on my new journey and replace my income within the first twelve months (insert eye roll here). I suffered from severe "compare-itis." I realized that I needed to unfollow certain people and start guarding my focus as if my life depended on it – which it does.

What's remained constant is my openness to opportunity and learning. I know that I have to be patient and continue to focus on my purpose, which is to use my passion and expertise to inspire and teach others to joyfully reach their highest potential.

I believe I was always afraid of losing the so-called "security" of my mortgage income. I also believe that it took every step of my forty-nine-year journey – the good, the bad and the ugly – to get to the point where I was ready to step into my power and purpose. Where I was ready to surrender to that quiet voice inside that had been speaking to me all along.

Today I know that I am meant to serve women in transition - whether it be professionally, personally, or spiritually.

I encourage you to listen to your own inner voice. Do the inner work necessary to get clear about why you are here.

And when you're feeling strong…LEAP!

Sheira's Tips for Showing Up *fashionably* LATE to:

Discovering and Embracing Your Purpose

- ۏ Invest in yourself – in doing the "inner work" necessary to live the life of your dreams.

- ۏ Save for any day, not just rainy ones. If you grow restless at any age, you'll want to have options.

- ۏ Let go of toxic, negative relationships and surround yourself with positive, supportive people.

- ۏ Don't compare your beginning to someone else's middle. Honor the process that is your life.

- ۏ Listen to your inner voice and get clear on your life's purpose.

Sheira MacKenzie

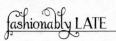

Part Two

Fitness and Hobbies

"There is a fountain of youth: it is your mind, your talents, the creativity you bring to your life and the lives of people you love. When you learn to tap this source, you will truly have defeated age."

Sophia Loren

I love this quote! Not only because of the message it offers, but also because of the spirit of the person who said it. Sophia Loren is a great example of someone who has ignored, or rather blown a sultry kiss at, conventional thinking on sex appeal.

Seriously, how fun is she, still rocking a cleavage dress well into her 70's?

Not interested in sex appeal? That's okay. Sophia isn't sexy because she's trying to be sexy. She's sexy because she's just being herself. She has embraced who she is and has refused to adapt how she shows up in the world simply because it isn't the norm.

You can do the same. Simply by embracing who you truly are and ignoring, or blowing a sultry kiss at, those who would judge you for it.

So be you. The best version of you that you can be. That's where life gets fun and interesting again. That's where life's magic is.

You're about to crack open a few chapters that will help you embrace the fashionably late concept as it pertains to your fitness and hobbies.

Some of the stories you'll find here are tales of hitting rock bottom mentally, physically and emotionally, and the struggle it took to come back from that. One story you'll read here is a tale of a long-lost dream of a child that the author had the courage to revive.

Whether you've struggled with your weight your entire life, or you used to feel healthy and fit, and now just feel like your body is deteriorating, or you've had a secret desire to take up some hobby or skill for a very long time and haven't yet made it happen, you'll be encouraged and inspired by what you read in this next section.

My son Corey, who is also my personal trainer, is very fond of saying that fitness begins in the mind. When you believe, deep down, that it's possible, and when you examine the dark thoughts that keep you from being your best self, you'll find that your fitness and personal goals are so much easier to achieve.

Allow these next chapters to plant the seed in your mind that perhaps it's not too late for you to lose those unwanted pounds, to become once again pain-free, or to learn a new skill – even a highly physical one.

Just for now, forget everything you've ever been told about your health, your body, your abilities, even the aging process in general. Instead, think thoughts like:

ᛗ My past doesn't predict my future. Just because I haven't done it before, doesn't mean I can't do it now.

ᛗ If fitness begins in the mind, mine is a clean slate, ready to be inspired by others who have achieved their goals.

ᛗ The only person who decides if I'm capable of something is me, and I'm prepared to believe I can master anything that brings me happiness.

ᛗ Genetics may have set a challenge before me, but I'm fully capable of overcoming any challenge I set my mind to.

No matter how long I've been harboring the desire to...

{fill in the blank},

fashionably LATE is better than showing up too early, and FAR better than never showing up at all!

Now, turn the page and let these authors convince you!

Amy Machacek is the founder and president of Life REVAMP, Inc. and HeartWork Studio, LLC. Highly energetic by nature with a passion for learning and teaching, Amy has completed many advanced coaching courses.

A certified health and nutrition coach with a degree from the Institute of Integrative Health, and a certified vinyasa yoga teacher, Amy has trained hundreds of yoga teachers through the school that she founded and has taught over 8,000 yoga classes. She holds a degree in Psychology and has been cited in numerous publications.

Amy has four grown children and lives in rural Minnesota. Her life's work is to hold a higher vision of a person until they can see and embody that for themselves.

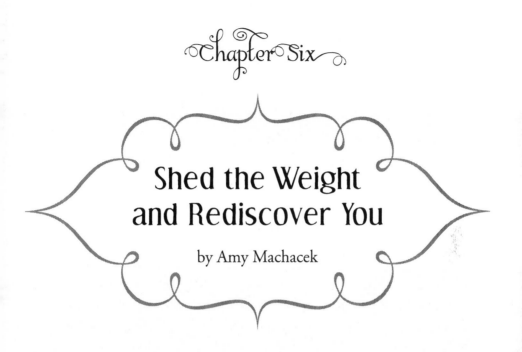

Chapter Six

Shed the Weight and Rediscover You

by Amy Machacek

"There is only one person responsible for where you are today."

Jack Canfield

I'm a fraud. The thought shot painfully through me as I stood in my bathroom, the fifth outfit I had tried on lying in a heap on the floor with the other discarded clothes.

All of my old standbys were in the pile. I had even tried on the swim suit from the summer my last baby was born. Having delivered a baby in March, I had caved and bought a larger-sized suit that summer.

Even that didn't feel good.

I felt like life had snuck away and taken my body with it.

Dejected, I turned from the mirror and sat on the edge of my clawfoot tub, the cast iron cold on the back of my legs. Perched on the edge in my underwear, I looked down at my body with annoyance. I wasn't in horrible shape, but the four pregnancies, all-too-often fast food dinners, and more-work-than-rest schedule I had been keeping for the past few years had definitely caught up with my once-thin body.

I got up from the tub, walked over to my scale and stepped on. When the numbers stopped climbing, I wanted to look away. The cold hard truth was that I had gained nearly 25 pounds in the past 12 years.

How did I get like this?

Slowly enough to go unnoticed, was my reply.

I had gained a couple of pounds every year for more than a decade. Funny, I remembered my mom telling me the same thing 25 years prior.

She had said, "It was three pounds at a time. Every time the scale went up, or my clothes got tight, I looked in the mirror and said, 'Oh, it's not so bad'."

Until the doctor's visit when the nurse wrote "obese" on her chart.

And there I was. An expert with years of training under my belt. I knew exactly what to do. Day after day, I instructed my clients on what to do. But I wasn't doing it myself, and that had to change. I was just over forty, and I felt horrible in my own skin.

At present, I was packing for a much-anticipated spa weekend with two girlfriends, and needed to bring a swimsuit and a couple of outfits for dinner and shopping.

Nothing was fitting.

Everything I tried on felt too tight and was binding in all the wrong places. I ended up tossing a few options into my bag and headed out.

Halfway into our three-hour drive, we stopped for lunch. As we left the restaurant, we stopped at their bakery counter to get a treat for the drive. My friends, deciding between a bagel or a pastry, each picked a bagel and walked out. I stepped up to the counter and, without thinking, ordered both a bagel and a pastry. As I turned to walk away, it occurred to me that this had become my norm.

The Cold, Hard Truth

Climbing back into the car, I was already deep in thought. I realized I was constantly overeating and under-exercising. I was saying "yes" to too many things that later brought a lot of resentment. I was constantly working to ensure my clients had the best of everything, which left no time for me. At home I was making sure the kids were cared for, the house was clean, and the projects were getting completed. I was an active volunteer at the kids' school and at church.

And I was a mess.

I went to work as a personal trainer, yoga teacher, and nutrition coach and taught my clients what and how to eat.

But I wasn't eating that way myself.

I instructed hundreds of yoga classes, but I wasn't doing much yoga.

I taught people how to lift weights to be healthy, but hadn't consistently lifted in a long time.

I talked to my clients about reducing their stress while continually taking on more and more in my own schedule.

My friendships were frail at best. I hadn't seen some of my "friends" in years. Could I really call them friends at this point? Probably not.

Frankly, I had stopped living and was simply working on getting through the day.

I did try.

Every week I'd buy veggies, only to throw them away ten days later because they had gone uneaten and were now rotten. I had heard that whole grains were good and, not yet knowing how damaging they are, ate a lot of them. My freezer was full of meat that I wasn't finding time to cook. My fridge was packed with food – things I wanted to make for my family. But usually, due to my lack of planning, dinner was quick pasta and sauce with garlic bread.

Every two weeks or so I'd by a twelve-pack of Coke™. At least once during that time, I'd say to my family, "I'm done drinking pop. I'm not going to buy it again." But on my next trip to the store, I'd do it all over again because I was always hungry and craving sugar. I was having this constant struggle of trying to stop, buying it again, wanting to avoid drinking it, and having no success.

I was keeping no personal commitments to myself.

I would start making time to work out and would be successful for a few days only to lapse for a week or more. Then I'd feel bad, and start again for a few days. But never really established a routine that stuck.

I would barely make it through the morning hours and then have to take a nap because I was eating so many nutrients that turned to sugar in my body. At work I would oftentimes go to my car to take a nap because I was so tired. I needed caffeine to simply get me through the day. And I consumed a lot of it.

The Plan

On the drive home from the spa weekend, I did something I'd never done before -- I shared with my friends how much I weighed.

It was an uneventful moment for them -- they didn't care how much I weighed. But for me, it felt like finally coming clean. My tall body can hide weight pretty easily, and declaring my weight out loud was like being transparent after a long period of hiding.

This conversation took place in late February. So tired of feeling unhealthy and exhausted, that very week I committed to making changes.

I started visualizing myself in a healthier body. I began eating to keep my blood sugar stable, which is what I had been teaching my clients. I started moving around and doing resistance training. I set a clear, measurable goal to once again see the 130's on the scale. I imagined in detail how that would feel. Every morning I would lie in bed, visualize myself walking down the street in this lighter, leaner body, and feel amazing.

I took workshops and read books on lower-carb, higher-fat eating. I would read the same book five or six times until I understood the science behind it. Then I'd experiment with eating that way. I watched YouTube™ videos and listened to podcasts. I tried new recipes. I took a handful of supplements each morning for more energy. I found a way to successfully add three liters of water into my day. I met my friends for walks rather than coffee.

And I visualized more and more, seeing myself in the body I knew was beneath the layer of fat.

And yes, I occasionally had a can of Coke™, a cupcake, or some pasta. I simply and consciously made it a treat, reminding myself that treats don't happen every day, but rather once or twice a week.

I also noticed how I felt the next morning after eating these things. Most often, I felt tired and cranky from eating all those carbs (which I now understood were simply turning into sugar in my body).

The Payoff

In late May, I decided to get away by myself for the weekend and returned to the same spa. I hadn't worn a bikini since college, but I packed one thinking I wouldn't know anyone anyway, so why not?

After lying by the spa pool, I stood up to leave…and glimpsed myself in the mirrored windows.

What I saw shocked me.

It was the body I used to know. My shoulders were defined; my waist narrow.

And it dawned on me. Four kids and 23 years after college, I felt better than ever. I no longer needed naps in the afternoon. I no longer felt shaky and starving two hours after eating.

I had been recording my weight every few days and knew it had gone down a lot, one pound most weeks, sometimes more. But I hadn't really been looking closely in the mirror, especially a full-length one. I work in a yoga and fitness studio, so I rarely wear anything but pull-on style athletic and yoga pants, which tend to hide weight fluctuations.

When I got home, I tried on my skinny pants and they were actually baggy. I shed five more pounds in the next couple of weeks to settle in the mid-130's, a weight I thought I'd never see again because of my age. I had released over 23 pounds, and I felt amazing!

The Purpose

I overhauled what I was teaching my fitness clients and went on to develop a program I call LIFE REVAMP. It combines fitness, nutrition, and goal setting into one complete, well-rounded six-week program.

Since then, hundreds of people have completed the program, so many of them shedding excess weight, and achieving physical, relationship, career and fitness goals.

I'm now sharing with others what I learned the hard way. I learned that I needed to do a few things consistently in order to shed weight and feel like myself again. These lessons include eating, sleeping, moving, lifting, breathing and seeing:

୬ *Eating* foods that keep my blood sugar stable.

୬ *Sleeping* at least seven hours a night.

୬ *Moving* my body at least twenty minutes most days of the week.

୬ *Lifting* my body weight or actual weights a couple times every week to build and maintain muscle.

୬ *Breathing* deeply every day to manage stress.

꼬 And finally, *seeing,* which is visualizing my goal as if it was already complete, in order to tap into the powerful emotion that comes with achieving it.

If it seems as if life has snuck away, taking your body with it, know that you can rediscover the real you. Begin with the simple belief that you can. Then make the decision that you will and commit to making some changes in your lifestyle.

Before long, you'll be feeling healthy, energetic and amazing!

Amy's Tips for Showing Up *fashionably* LATE for:
An Amazing, Healthy Life

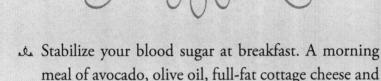

- Stabilize your blood sugar at breakfast. A morning meal of avocado, olive oil, full-fat cottage cheese and sliced tomatoes with salt and pepper is excellent. This will keep your blood sugar stable and keep you full for hours.

- Aim to sweat for twenty minutes at least four times per week. Twenty minutes consistently helps a lot.

- Drink two to three liters of water a day. Staying hydrated keeps you feeling awake and energetic.

- Do the things that bring you joy. Be mindful of the things in your life you're grateful for. Remember to connect with your friends, spend time in nature, and laugh often.

Connie Whitesell is the founder of *Scattered to Streamlined.* Through her business planning and coaching services, Connie is devoted to helping business owners and executives live their professional dreams.

Have you ever been in a situation where you have seemingly hundreds of different ideas floating around in your head about experiences you wish to have and goals you want to reach? It is exciting to think about the possibilities, but may also be overwhelming figuring out where to begin and how to focus your efforts. That's where Connie comes in. She coaches individuals, helping them take those brilliant, but often scattered, ideas and streamline them into plans, systems, and habits that support them in achieving their objectives.

Fifty and Falling Apart

A Lesson in Body Awareness

by Connie Whitesell

"…and I said to my body, softly, 'I want to be your friend'.
It took a long breath, and replied,
'I have been waiting my whole life for this.'"

Nayyira Waheed

In 2015, I turned *fifty and my body said "No More."* My husband Jim and I (and our two wonderful old pups) moved to Buffalo in 2015 for Jim's new basketball coaching job at University at Buffalo. Having moved several times in the previous five years, you would think we would be used to it.

Not quite.

As with any basketball job, the coach moves immediately upon hire. In our case, Jim moved in May while I remained in Long

---

Beach, New York, to work out the logistics of our move…and to enjoy as many remaining walks along the ocean as I could.

Once again, we were separated, making long drives on weekends to be together while scrambling to find a new home in an area where the housing market was booming and definitely preferred the sellers.

Buffalo - who knew?!

It all worked out. We moved into our beautiful one-hundred-year-old home in July and began renovations. A month or so of dust, unpacked boxes, workers throughout the house – and then we settled in.

A few people, including our sellers, told us air conditioning was unnecessary in Buffalo.

They lied.

We sweated our way through July and August, eventually giving in to window units upstairs.

While Jim settled in to his new job, I set about getting to know our new area and meeting new people. For this, I had developed a knack.

Not finding a hiking group I enjoyed, I started my own.

Couldn't find a book club group. Started my own.

Looked for a networking group but could not find one that appealed to me. Started one.

I was not about to wait. Who knew how long we would be here?

I run two businesses, a business coaching practice and a human resources consulting firm. While I adore my individual coaching clients, I also felt it was important to focus on scaling my business

– offering more group and online options that would travel with me a bit better than my one-on-one work.

On to writing my book and developing new offerings – a group coaching program and an online course.

Hey, why not throw in a workshop series offered out of my home?!

A good friend and colleague asked me whether I was interested in being an author in a book collaboration. My accountability partner and I decided to move forward with our idea to develop a retreat for women in some fabulous locale. A desire to reconnect with my Jack Canfield training community led me to volunteer to assist with two weeks of 2016 in-person training sessions as well as provide guidance to a monthly mastermind group.

Falling Apart

In December, I hit a milestone birthday – the big 5-0. And, for the first time...did not embrace my age.

The holidays arrived. Basketball season was in full swing. Tragedy hit – Jim's funny, kind, loving, amazingly-dedicated-to-following-his-dreams younger brother passed away after eighteen months of suffering with brain cancer.

Jim and I were traveling, grieving, and doing our best to hold things together. Except my body wasn't.

December began for me with intense knee pain and a stiffening shoulder. By this point, I was hiking almost every morning, leading a daily sunrise "hike to health" series and doing my best – unsuccessfully – to take off several extra pounds that had crept in over the past year.

My doctor told me the cartilage in my knees was mostly gone, leaving my knees bone-on-bone. A fall exacerbated the problem with my left knee, leaving me unable to hike or walk any long distance. My right shoulder became "frozen," a ridiculously painful condition. I began a regimen of physical therapy for the knee and shoulder, to no avail.

The shoulder pain was unresponsive to any of the numerous medications prescribed to me. Shots didn't help. The pain kept me sleeping no more than three hours each night. Prolonged taking of pain medication caused my stomach to revolt and brought on its own set of issues. A weakened system left me open to a nasty bout of the stomach flu.

None of this was life-threatening. People suffer far worse than I have. But, by March of 2016, my lifestyle had completely changed.

I was no longer hiking, one of my biggest passions. I had to cancel important trips, including a much anticipated family visit to California, the first round of the NCAA Tournament to see my husband's team play, and going to Chicago for a new client meeting and to visit mom and dad for the Easter holiday. It was tough to leave home due to the pain, not sleeping, and not knowing when my stomach would give me trouble.

Finally it hit me. What was my body trying to tell me?

As I write this, it seems so obvious. But I couldn't see it.

I wasn't slowing down, so my body forced me to stop entirely. I could hear Oprah Winfrey's often-repeated quote: "Difficulties come when you don't pay attention to life's whisper. Life always whispers to you first, but if you ignore the whisper, sooner or later you'll get a scream."

My body was screaming.

What to do?

The good thing was that a gel injection helped my knee, and surgery in early April began the process of un-freezing my shoulder. A long regimen of physical therapy was to come, but at least I could finally wash my hair – with both hands!

Beyond the physical work, however, I realized that more of a life change was needed to ensure continued healing and to keep these issues from recurring. Before this, I never could have imagined that a shoulder issue could cause so much pain for such a prolonged period and I knew that I never wanted to go through that, or anything like it, again.

Putting Me Back Together Again

Drastic change was needed and this is what it looked like:

Professionally:

- I reviewed my 2016 business plan and ruthlessly slashed projects and activities, many of which were intended to grow my business, including cancelling:
  - my home-based workshop series group
  - a mastermind program I was just about to launch
  - my leadership and attendance at local networking groups
  - my attendance at the Canfield program.

- I postponed the development of my online course and the writing of my book.

꘠ I decided that when it came to my coaching business, I would focus entirely on providing exceptional service to my one-on-one coaching clients and nothing else.

꘠ In the interest of winding down my Human Resources consulting business, I told my largest client, a large Chicago-based government agency, that I would not be re-bidding on the project contract at the end of the year.

Personally:

꘠ Just before surgery, Jim and I found a secluded cabin in the Adirondacks where we spent a few days relaxing – wandering through the snow along a peaceful stream, reading, enjoying slow-cooked meals with delicious wine.

꘠ I slowed down my leadership activities with the hiking group and asked others to help fill the gaps.

꘠ I did my best to keep every weekend and most evenings free and unplanned.

꘠ I took daily naps.

꘠ I signed up for a weekly food delivery service that provided the ingredients and recipes for healthy and delicious meals.

꘠ I said "no" to any invitation or opportunity that left me feeling stressed or overbooked.

Fifty and Fabulous

By June 2016, six months after the start of my physical breakdown, my life had changed completely.

Professionally:

- I had more one-on-one coaching clients than ever before.

- With more time and focus, I provided better service to my clients, resulting in much more deep and satisfying connections.

- I began enjoying the process of contributing to the book compilation and planning the retreat instead of feeling stressed out about having way too many projects on my plate.

- My income increased from both of my businesses.

- My stress level decreased significantly.

Personally:

- I felt a marked improvement in my physical health. My knee no longer bothered me and my shoulder was almost back to normal.

- I began leading hikes again. Other group organizers had kept hikes going and providing such a wide variety of activities (full moon hikes, frog "concerts," orienteering events – ideas that never would have come to me alone). I was hardly missed! Our group grew from six hundred to eight hundred while I was gone and, when I returned, I could do so leading hikes on a less frequent, more enjoyable schedule.

❧ I could travel again without fear of pain limiting me.

❧ My love of fiction reading was rekindled and enjoyed.

❧ I enjoyed much more leisurely time with my husband - going for drives in our '65 Mustang convertible, exploring our new hometown, or just playing gin rummy on our front porch.

❧ I did more spontaneous things like crossing the border to Canada (twenty minutes away) and enjoying lunch with a friend on her beautiful deck overlooking Lake Erie – on a Tuesday!

❧ I regularly slept through the night. For that I was most grateful.

My body sent a clear, painful, and ultimately life-changing message. I now know that maintaining my emotional, mental, and physical health has to be my top and ongoing priority.

What may your body be trying to tell you?

Are you listening?

Connie's Tips for Arriving *fashionably* LATE for:

A Healthy Lifestyle through Body Awareness

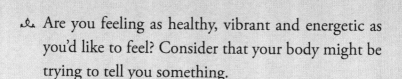

ᒧ Are you feeling as healthy, vibrant and energetic as you'd like to feel? Consider that your body might be trying to tell you something.

ᒧ Find a quiet place to sit for a few minutes, close your eyes and ask your body to tell you what you need to know.

ᒧ Realize that physical discomforts and conditions might be indicators of mental and emotional stress, as well as physical stress.

ᒧ Learn to get comfortable saying "no" to requests that make you feel stressed or overbooked.

ᒧ Know that you may find more fulfillment in life simply by slowing down, doing less and focusing on those activities you truly love.

Tricia Guerra is a physician assistant (PA) living outside of Dallas, Texas, with her husband René and three cats. She specializes in diabetes and lipid disorders at the North Texas VA Medical Center, working with military veterans. She came fashionably late to her profession as a PA, changing careers in her mid-thirties. She has achieved Advanced Communicator Gold Level in her Toastmasters® Club, is a certified HeartMath® trainer and coach, and completed Jack Canfield's Train the Trainer program. Her priority is to cherish and be fully present in each moment. Passionate about service to others, she is ready to explore opportunities to serve outside of medicine, where she may use her own unique blend of skills, wisdom and experience.

Chapter Eight

Age is a Number, Not an Excuse

by Tricia Guerra

"When you are inspired, you no longer need motivation."

Andy Shaw

Like many young girls, I dreamed of riding a horse. In my romantic daydreams, I saw myself on a horse galloping across a pasture covered in wildflowers, my long hair blowing in the wind.

But it was not to be, not at that time.

After my father died when I was only seven, my mother struggled to make ends meet on her own. I didn't have the heart to ask for riding lessons, because I knew she would sacrifice yet something else she needed in order to make it happen.

As life went on, my dream became increasingly distant. I graduated from high school and college, got married and divorced, changed careers, got happily remarried, and became active in my career and professional organization. Thoughts of horses grew even more remote.

As I entered my forties, I began to view life differently and to examine my priorities. I was no longer interested in wasting my precious energy or time on activities for which I had no passion. Slowly, my connection to horses resurfaced.

Around that time, I became friends with a woman named Kathy.

She owned two horses and had many connections with people in the local horse community. She introduced me to a trainer, Christine, and my journey into the equestrian world began.

A Seven-Year-Old Finally Gets Her Wish

At the age of forty-nine, I drove to my first lesson with a mixture of excited anticipation and sheer terror. I had serious doubts about my ability to do this.

I am not naturally athletic, so I had concerns about my capacity to learn a new skill that required coordination, balance and athleticism. I knew there was a serious risk of exposing myself as the "klutz" I have always considered myself.

Then Christine introduced me to the horse I was to ride.

His name was RC, short for Real Cool Dude, and I was in love. I desperately wanted to be connected to this magnificent animal that had such a sweet spirit. I was willing to do whatever it took to learn to ride him.

Tricia Guerra

This decision was not easy for me. I'm a perfectionist who rarely tries anything new unless there's an excellent chance of doing it well.

I found the simplest of tasks, like putting the halter on his head correctly or tying a rope, to be embarrassingly challenging. I often found myself humiliated by the mistakes I would make, especially since I seemed to repeat them endlessly. Even worse, these blunders were often public, as I was usually surrounded by an audience of other riders in addition to my instructor. But I wanted this so badly that I persevered. Gradually, my skills improved.

Then life once again got in the way.

My mother's health started to decline and she began her descent into dementia. Taking care of her so that she could remain in her own home required more and more of my time. Though it was difficult, there was really no other choice I would have made. I gave up my riding lessons in order to devote my time to my mother.

But I never gave up my dream.

Committing to the Dream

At this same time, my friend Kathy was dealing with her own challenges, having been diagnosed with late stage breast cancer. As the cancer progressed, she began to talk to me about one day taking her younger horse, Shanti. When I could, I would steal away and visit Shanti in her pasture, just sitting with her and occasionally doing some groundwork with her.

Ultimately, Kathy made the difficult decision to find new homes for Shanti and her mother Sheffara. She was firm in her desire that mother and daughter leave the property at the same time. Since she had already found a home for Sheffara, I had little time to consider my options. If I didn't decide soon, she would find another home for Shanti and she would be lost to me.

My mind swirled with doubts. The child in me had wanted this her whole life; the logical adult was afraid of what this commitment entailed. My heart said yes. I moved Shanti to a boarding facility and our life together began.

Back in the Saddle

Ten-year-old Shanti was untrained, mentally immature, moody and highly opinionated – a poor choice for an amateur. It quickly became apparent that Shanti needed training that I wasn't qualified to provide. Fortunately, my friend Colette, a highly-regarded and experienced trainer, was willing to take both of us under her wing. A highly intelligent horse, Shanti quickly progressed in her training.

I, however, am still a work in progress.

Despite Colette's patient training, I again confronted my demons of perfectionism, little athletic ability, and the reality that learning a new, highly physical skill at an older age is more difficult.

I would often leave my lessons in frustration and despair, wondering if I was just too inept. Riding became even more difficult as I developed chronic pain from osteoarthritis in both knees. Every step I took was excruciating. The constant pain stretched me to my limit – physically, mentally and emotionally.

Shanti's personality presented its own challenges. She had little patience for my lack of skill. People told me that I simply needed to "be a leader" to her and she would respect me. As a lifelong leader in my life and my work, I was baffled by this advice. I didn't understand what that meant in regard to horses. This proved to be another source of frustration, and only reinforced my belief that I was inadequate.

I shed many tears, oftentimes in self-pity, about my relationship with Shanti. I struggled with the belief that I was just not good enough for her. I loved her; yet I was desperately afraid of failing her.

The turning point came when my mother's death caused me to again re-examine my life. My own mortality was becoming much more real to me. Then one of my favorite spiritual teachers, Dr. Wayne Dyer, died at age seventy-five, only sixteen years older than me. His passing reinforced for me that I absolutely must live my remaining life to the fullest.

I was finally ready to put my thoughts of failure and inadequacy aside, "get over myself" and get on with life.

Self-Care, Awareness and Lessons Animals Can Teach Us

Instead, I focused on taking care of myself, something I had neglected during the time I was caring for Mother. I started taking riding lessons again, and had both of my knees replaced so that pain no longer interfered with riding and caring for my horse.

I have always believed that the animals in our lives are here to provide us with life lessons. Shanti is no exception. One of the most important principles in horsemanship is to establish and maintain boundaries with your horse.

As an introvert who lost my father at a young age, I have had a lifelong fear of rejection and abandonment. This created in me a reluctance to speak my truth, to stand up for myself, and to have strong boundaries with others.

Forcing me to face these doubts and fears so that I am comfortable with having strong boundaries seems to be Shanti's purpose in my life.

I now manage doubt-ridden self-talk and perfectionism by being present and aware of my thoughts, questioning their validity. Being a "work in progress" has been hard for this perfectionist to accept, so "progress, not perfection" has become my new mantra. Learning to ride a horse, like most other things in life, is not a destination but a journey that will never end. Though I can now ride capably, I will always learn more about riding, and about myself, if I stay open to it.

While acquiring a new skill such as horseback riding at an older age can truly be more challenging, the belief that I am "too old" is simply not true, regardless of age.

Sadly, many of us use this false belief, and others like it, as an excuse for staying inside of our comfort zones, and avoiding living our dreams.

The Importance of Feedback

One of the greatest lessons I've learned in this process is the importance of being open to feedback. When former Dallas Cowboy Emmitt Smith won Dancing with the Stars, he was asked how being a professional athlete contributed to his victory. His response was that participating in sports taught him to be coachable.

That has been my experience in my journey with Shanti.

When I was faced with the daunting task of learning to ride a horse like Shanti, I put myself completely into my trainer's hands. In this age of instant access to information, it's tempting to rely solely on electronic resources to educate ourselves, forgoing the advice of an experienced expert. But feedback about yourself and your performance is critical for growth. The internet can't replace having a coach observe you and provide insight and instruction.

While I could read and watch videos about riding, those are no substitute for the individual feedback from my experienced trainer. I can't count the number of times I thought my hands or legs were in the proper position, yet Colette pointed out that they were doing something else entirely.

Regardless of the skill you're learning, never underestimate the power of feedback. And being coachable makes being outside of your comfort zone much easier.

In spite of the frustration, I've had many moments of pure joy and exhilaration while riding. Passion is what gets me back on my horse, time and time again, even though I don't know what will be in store for the ride that day. Without passion, I could easily have given in to the belief that I was too old to learn how to ride.

I don't know where my journey with Shanti will take me, or where it will end. She is still a difficult horse who challenges the limits of my skill and erodes my confidence. But, whatever may happen with her, I won't stop riding. I've discovered my passion.

Reaching new goals requires dedication and persistence. But without passion and strong desire, you end up relying on willpower, which can fade. When your desire is strong, you become inspired. As Wayne Dyer said in his book, Excuses Begone!, *"Passion always trumps excuses."*

When I have been tempted to give in to the excuse that I'm too old to learn this, my passion for riding and love for my horse keeps me going.

Whatever your vision is, approach it with passion, inspiration and the support of others. Age may need to be a consideration, but never allow it to keep you from doing what you're passionate about!

Tricia's Tips for Showing Up *fashionably* LATE for:
Learning a New Skill

- Manage negative self-talk by being present and aware of your thoughts; question their validity.

- Progress, Not Perfection" is a helpful mantra while learning a new skill.

- Feedback is critical while learning a new skill, so don't go it alone. Enlist the help of someone who's skilled at doing what you're trying to learn.

- Anticipate frustration while you're learning, and know that the joy will make it all worth it.

- Approach your goal with passion, inspiration and the support of others.

- If you're not passionate about your goal, re-consider if this is really right for you.

- Age may be a consideration, but never allow it to keep you from your dream.

Danne Reed is a best-selling author, entrepreneur, founder and CEO of fashionably LATE Productions, LLC, and the fashionably LATE Foundation, and founder and creator of ProWoRC, a community and conference for Professional Women of Rural Communities.

She's on a mission to encourage people that it's never too late to rediscover and embrace their passions and talents, and that opportunities abound wherever you are.

Danne believes that we are each deserving of our dream life and that with a few simple, yet profound twists, that dream life can be ours.

You can connect with Danne at *DanneReed.com* and *ProWoRC.com*.

Chapter Nine

Finding My Hallelujah!

by Danne Reed

"Vincit Que Se Vincit."
Latin phrase meaning:
"She conquers, who conquers herself."

Vincit, que se vincit. Vincit, que se vincit. I repeated the phrase over and over and over in my mind as I plodded along on the hot, winding sidewalk, each placement of my feet, one after the other, a sheer act of will now that my forty-one-year-old body had reached its physical limit for the day.

I was on the homestretch of my first solo triathlon, having completed my first tri the year before, at the age of forty, as part of a relay team. There was no one to take the "baton" from me this time. I was on my own and feeling every step of it.

I was in author Darryl Rosen's "middle miles" that I mentioned in the introduction, referring to the part of a marathon or race that consists of the space between the excitement of the gun sounding the start, and the enormous rush of relief and joy of getting that first awesome glimpse of the finish line up ahead.

It's the part where your preparation and training – physical and mental -- such as they are, come into play in the most intense way.

And as any endurance athlete will confirm, the physical training will only take you so far. Being prepared mentally is every bit as critical as the physical training, if not more so.

It's not always the first thing you think of when you commit to completing a race or other physical feat.

When I first decided I wanted to do a triathlon, I focused almost exclusively on the physical aspect of getting ready:

- I put together a plan to make sure I was practicing each event at least twice a week – swimming, running, biking.

- I researched proper nutrition for training for a tri and incorporated new eating habits, tracking my intake meticulously.

- I added some strength training to my weekly schedule.

- I increased my daily water intake to account for the loss during all of this exercise.

Not knowing what to expect, I followed a few guidelines for staying on track:

☙ I registered early for the event, so that the goal was firm and I was less likely to back out.

☙ I told friends and family what I was doing, again so that I was less likely to back out.

☙ I found an accountability partner, again, less likely to back out…

Are you noticing a pattern?

Yep, that was apparently a major concern for me, though I wasn't consciously aware of it at the time.

Looking back, it's clear that I believed the biggest threat to not finishing the race was that I would "chicken out" before even showing up.

I didn't give a second thought to that space of time after the start of the race, and before I could see the finish line.

And this, my friend, is where the true challenge lies. Because the more exhausted you are and the farther you are outside of your comfort zone (literally in dis-comfort), the more likely you are to see inside yourself and face your own demons, which are ultimately nothing more than your own fears and doubts.

In completing other physically demanding feats, such as hiking to the summits of Pikes Peak and Mount Elbert in Colorado, I've discovered that the mental pattern – the logical and emotional process that I go through – is the same, regardless of the actual challenge.

And this is how it inevitably goes:

Step One: The Idea Phase, or Courtship.

This is where the idea and I cross paths. I'm attracted to the idea, so I pay it lots of attention, learning all I can about it and convincing myself that the idea and I would make a great couple. This was the phase where I fell in love with the idea of completing a triathlon.

Step Two: The Commitment Phase, or The Wedding.

This is usually a pretty quick phase, where I commit to the idea with all my heart and soul. I set a goal to make the idea a part of my life, whatever it is, 'til death do us part. I wrote down the goal to complete a triathlon, registered for an upcoming event and told some friends that I was doing it.

Step Three: The Start Up Phase, or Honeymoon.

I'm so excited to make my idea a reality that I eagerly dive in, confident that I'm fully prepared to enjoy the entire process. Notice that it's now my idea, rather than the idea. During my Honeymoon with my triathlon idea, I kicked it into gear with exercise and meal plans, and eagerness to work out each day.

Step Four: The Initial Snag, or Our First Disagreement.

I run into the first major obstacle in the path towards my idea. It's okay, I tell myself here, you weren't expecting all smooth-sailing, right? I work my way around the Initial Snag and carry on, feeling quite proud of myself for not giving up at the first sign of trouble. For example, during one of my early biking sessions, I threw my lower back out of place (since I hadn't been on a bike for years). It was several days before I could move around without pain.

Step Five: The Plodding Along Phase, or The Honeymoon's Definitely Over.

By now, I've gotten into a routine with my idea, following along under a plan I created long ago. I've achieved minor milestones along the way, but that initial spark of excitement has long since faded to a dull ember of hope that maybe someday I'll achieve my idea.

On the path to my first solo triathlon, the long stretch of regular exercise and healthy nutrition became tedious at times. And, of course, there was that part during the race when my body had had enough.

Step Six: The Tipping Point, or The Huge Fight.

Somewhere along the way, the fear suddenly grips me that maybe rather than me having the idea, the idea is having me.

The excitement gone, major obstacles now begin to look like stop signs, rather than challenges to overcome.

In my mind, I begin to justify throwing the entire idea out, and start fantasizing about how easy and great my life might be if the idea and I simply parted ways, as friends, of course. This is the part of the process where I'm at my lowest, where my fears and self-doubts grab me by the throat and growl at me to quit before something really bad happens, like totally embarrassing myself.

Step Seven: The Return of Excitement Phase, or Makeup Sex After the Huge Fight.

This is where I remember why I really wanted this idea in my life to begin with. Like I did in the beginning, or Courtship phase, I visualize and think about how great my life will be once I've achieved the goal. The catalyst for this phase cannot be predicted. I never know from where this inspiration will come.

Step Eight: The Re-Commitment Phase, or Renewing My Vows.

I refocus on the goal, rather than the obstacles like I've had a tendency to do during the Plodding Along, or Honeymoon's Definitely Over, Phase.

Note here that Steps 5 through 8 may be repeated again and again, depending on how big the idea or lengthy the goal.

Now before I go on, let me take you back to that hot summer day, and there I am, smack in the middle of the Honeymoon's-Definitely-Over phase of my idea to complete my first solo triathlon, and the mental garbage begins bubbling to the surface of my mind, like noxious fumes boiling from an old witch's cauldron (the Tipping Point or Huge Fight):

"You aren't up to this; you should just quit and try again some other day."

"Look at all of these other younger, more fit competitors. You're too old and out of shape."

"Why are you doing this? This is a lot of pain and agony, and for what?"

"It's not like you're getting paid to do it, and you're certainly not going to win."

"It's just like you to get these wild ideas and then fizzle out once the excitement has passed. Are you ever going to follow through on anything..."

"Man, this sucks. Triathlons suck. My fitness level sucks. In fact, what really sucks is…" Suddenly, the voice of a complete stranger interrupts my inner dialog, "Looking good, Number 632!! Keep going; you're almost there!"

And there it was – the catalyst for the Return of Excitement phase. I'll admit it – I got a little teary-eyed. This guy, this random, total stranger is nicer to me than I am.

I refocus and begin anew repeating my mantra in cadence with the pounding of my footfalls on the pavement…

"Vincit que se vincit."

"She conquers who conquers herself..."

"Don't give up. Don't give in. The desire to quit is temporary; the fears and doubts will fade."

"Finishing the race will last a lifetime."

And suddenly, I see in the distance up ahead, the finish line, surrounded by cheering crowds and professional athletes high-fiving everyone as they sprint or stumble across the line.

Fueled by sheer will and the encouraging words of a stranger who will never know the part he played, I muster the last of my strength and cross the finish line – closer to the stumble end of the sprint/stumble spectrum – and yes, with the damned tears in my eyes for the second time that day, but I finish. I did it!

Which brings me to...

Step Nine: The Hallelujah Phase, or Blissful Marriage!

I've finally achieved what I set out to do. The idea has become a part of me, a part of who I am, and I couldn't be happier or more fulfilled. I'm living my life on a whole new level that I didn't dream possible before.

And then, from that elevated place...I start thinking...maybe I could do an Ironman...

Danne's Tips for Showing Up *fashionably* LATE for:

Practically Anything!

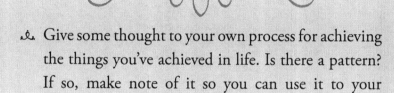

- Give some thought to your own process for achieving the things you've achieved in life. Is there a pattern? If so, make note of it so you can use it to your advantage in achieving other goals.

- Don't mistake your *Honeymoon's Definitely Over Phase* for an indication that it's time to give up the idea. Trust your intuition to tell you whether it's still an idea worth pursuing.

- Be open to encouragement and inspiration from any source; it might even be the words of a stranger that fuel you to renew your focus.

- It ain't over until you say it is. Regardless of how long you've been stuck in the *Honeymoon's Definitely Over Phase,* or how many times you've *Renewed Your Vow* to the idea, you can still achieve it, as long as you keep moving toward your goal and don't give up.

- No matter how long it takes, the *Hallelujah Phase* is worth the effort! Don't lose sight of the dream while you're working toward it. Stop and visualize it every chance you get; these mini-daydreams will sustain you until your dream becomes a reality.

Part
Three

Part Three

Personal Challenges

"And the day came when the risk to remain tight in a bud was more painful than the risk it took to blossom."

Anaïs Nin

Have you ever felt that if something in your life didn't change, and change quick, you were going to explode? Or implode? Or have a nervous breakdown? Or at the very least, seriously lose your cool for bit?

I think we've all experienced a point in our lives when the status quo just wasn't going to work for us anymore, and we knew that something had to give. As the quote above so eloquently states – it's more painful to keep doing what we've been doing than it would be to make a change.

And we all know how scary and painful change can be.

In my first book in the fashionably LATE series – *Fashionably Late: A Sexy Little Twist to Revitalize You and ReDesign Your Life!* – I talk about how there came a time in my life when I was becoming resentful, bitter and simply uncomfortable in my own skin. It was a journey of several years, and more than a few emotional shake-ups, that brought me to the realization that I was at the heart of my discomfort and unhappiness.

Prior to that, it was a comfortable habit for me to lay the blame for my unhappiness at the feet of those around me, particularly my husband.

Initially, the thought that I was contributing to my own unhappiness was fairly painful to even consider. Every fiber of my being wanted to rebel against the idea that it was "my fault." But as I learned and grew in my knowledge of personal transformation, I eventually began to see it as the hidden treasure that it is. If I was causing my own unhappiness, then I, and I alone, could fix it, right?

If this idea is new to you, you may be wanting to chuck this book into the garbage right about now.

Don't do it just yet!

First, I want you to ask yourself a few questions:

- Is it possible that you're feeling pain or discomfort because you're not quite living your life at your full potential?

- Is there any area of your life – whether it's in your relationships, or your work, your finances, or anything else – where you feel like you could be doing better, or even deserve better?

ℒ And if either of those are possible, could it also be possible that there are things, even little things, that you could do to move yourself closer to living your full potential?

Those are questions that the authors in this section asked themselves after a period of struggling with emotional pain and/or turmoil. At some point, they took a step back to examine their lives and question the possibilities. That's all you need to do to begin moving in an empowering direction – consider the possibilities.

The next step is also a simple one – consider the idea that "pain is inevitable; suffering is optional." No one seems to know for sure where this phrase came from, but it's incredibly profound. Where emotional pain is acute and urgent, like the grief we feel when we lose a loved one, suffering implies that we've somehow gotten stuck in that emotional pain.

And there are many degrees of suffering.

Motivational speaker Tony Robbins invites people to consider all emotions on the negative end of the spectrum, such as frustration, resentment, anger, and sadness, as forms of suffering. And while these are all natural human emotions, they do have a "shelf life" and are not meant to be permanent conditions.

One of my favorite spiritual mentors, Dr. Deb Sandella, encourages people to think of negative emotions like water flowing in a river. If we allow our emotions to flow, thereby acknowledging the feelings and allowing them to exist, they will naturally dissipate. It is when we "dam" the river up that the emotions can get stuck inside of us and take up a more permanent residence in our psyche.

To live this way, with "dams" built up inside our minds and our hearts, is to never fully live. By locking these emotions up inside, we hold pieces of ourselves back from the world, from our relationships, from ourselves.

In this way, a person who experiences a breakup of a relationship, but doesn't allow themselves to feel sadness or hurt over it – perhaps hiding the pain behind bravado – may enter into their next relationship with a subconscious goal of not getting too attached.

They could easily and unknowingly sabotage the new relationship by keeping the other person at arm's length, in order to avoid pain over the next breakup.

Like many of us, the authors in this section of the book know what it's like to live with a part of themselves held back from the world, from their relationships, from themselves. They experienced the condition of "not fully living" and decided not to stay in that state.

The stories in this section may initially sadden and anger, disturb, and perhaps even shock you. In these chapters, you'll find sadness and grief, loneliness and heartache.

There is trauma here – physical and emotional – and unfathomable betrayal.

And yet, none of these stories end there.

Like all of the authors in the book, through cleverness and humor, creativity, courage, and sheer strength of will, each of the authors in this section found a way to overcome.

Each in their own way began to consider the possibility that there was something better.

Each in their own way recognized that they were suffering, that the pain or discomfort they were experiencing was lingering, and that they deserved better for themselves and their loved ones.

And each in their own way, chose to make a change.

As with all hero's journeys, the most profound battles take place internally – in the heart and mind of the hero herself.

Turn the page, and let these courageous women inspire you to recognize the hero inside of you...

CJ Paulus is a 51-year-old proud single mother of three sons.

In her spare time, she loves to transform tired, worn-out, forgotten items into beautiful creations. She has a lifelong dream of illustrating a children's book she wrote many years ago.

She loves connecting with, encouraging and inspiring others whether it's a stranger or a long-time friend or family member.

She is currently rediscovering herself and her mission in life.

CJ is a Tradeshow Planner for a pharmaceutical company and is in the process of determining what her next career will be.

Chapter Ten

My Happily Ever After

by CJ Paulus

O tested soul, perhaps the Lord is sending you through this trial to develop your gifts. You have some gifts that would never have been discovered if not for trials. Do you not know that your faith never appears as great in the warm summer weather does during a cold winter? Your love is all too often like a firefly, showing very little light except when surrounded by darkness. And hope is like the stars – unseen in the sunshine of prosperity and only discovered during a night of adversity. Afflictions are often the dark settings God uses to mount the jewels of His children's gifts, causing them to shine even brighter.
L.B. Cowman

When I was just three years old, I developed and was hospitalized for a severe case of pneumonia. This happened at a time when parents were not allowed in the room while the doctor performed his examination.

I remember my Mother telling me how traumatic it was for her to be physically removed from the hospital room while I was screaming for her not to leave me. I don't remember much about this time other than being alone in a small oxygen tent cut off from my family and the rest of the world.

The hospital also had a "no children allowed" visitor policy. Thus, my only link to my siblings during my hospital stay was through get-well wishes in the form of pictures they had drawn for me.

Holding the drawings in my hands, I felt the love that had gone into creating each one.

Reflecting back on this in my later years, I believe this was when I developed a deep love of connecting with people through drawing and works of creation. It's probably also when I developed my lifelong struggle with claustrophobia, but that's a story for another day.

As a little girl, I dreamed of writing, illustrating and publishing children's books. And yet, after graduating from high school, I went to work full-time, started a family and concentrated on providing, believing deep-down that publishing children's books was an impossible dream.

I've drawn throughout my entire life although I've never made a living at it. I wrote my first children's book more than twenty years ago and spent the next twenty years with a serious case of creative block and what I accepted as procrastination.

My talent basically remained on the shelf except for special occasions and holidays when my inspiration and lifelong passion would break through. I felt wonderful and fulfilled when doing anything creative, whether it was drawing pictures for children, making garage sale signs, making a special meal, decorating a cake or cookies for my family or friends, or just making anything that looked tired and worn into something beautiful.

It's difficult to describe the subtle shift that occurs in a child's mood, or the faint stirring of imagination that flickers in their eyes when they observe something being created just for them. Many times, I captured a moment of a child's life, with them looking on.

As I drew them from my perspective – cute, fun, worthy of the attention and adoration – I could sense when their own perspective of themselves shifted as well. In this way, much like all of my creative endeavors, my artistic gift served as a bridge, connecting me to the recipient in a way that wouldn't have been possible without it.

These occasional, profound connections were islands of joy-filled creativity in the otherwise task-oriented sea of my life.

I continued this way, largely ignoring the urge to create and share my gifts with others, until my mid-forties when life as I knew it began to change.

My life was drastically altered through the loss of my mother, the dissolution of my fourteen-year marriage and the sale of my home at a huge loss to avoid foreclosure.

It was several years before I regained my emotional and financial stability, and I spent an exorbitant amount of time dreaming about my knight in shining armor who would take me away from all my worries.

A Journey

In November of 2014, I began a journey of discovery when I attended a retreat in Colorado Springs hosted by Danne Reed. The transformation didn't happen overnight, however, I did become aware of a new possibility.

Maybe my dreams were more than just dreams. Maybe they were the key to my happiness.

I also learned to share my thoughts, dreams and fears with others. I used to keep all of my faults to myself for fear people wouldn't approve of me. I was reluctant to share my dreams for fear someone might either take them or discourage me from pursuing them. I became better equipped to decipher when to listen to someone else's advice and when to ignore it. I began to seek and receive messages from every possible source, trusting my intuition when something felt right for me. These messages were always there; I had just been looking the other way!

One powerful example is a statement I heard one morning while watching TV: *"Happiness is the joy we feel growing towards our potential."*

I realized I had been viewing the steps to obtaining my dream as impassable obstacles and sheer drudgery. I didn't see them as the rewarding, invigorating, life-changing learning experiences they really are.

Getting Lost, and Found Again

I was so honored and excited when I was asked to contribute to this book. However, after a few days of further thought and without any knowledge of the other authors, I started feeling extremely intimidated and completely inadequate. My thoughts were along the lines of:

"I haven't achieved any of my goals in life. I'm not financially stable. I haven't published a children's book. I haven't found my happily ever after. I'm not living in the cabin on the lake. What do I really have to offer?"

The poet Robert Frost said *"the best way out is always through."*

So I trudged through the fear and self-doubt I was experiencing to really examine the source of these thoughts, and whether there was any validity to the idea that I hadn't achieved any of my goals.

And I discovered something.

Not only have I achieved many of my goals, but, without my being consciously aware of it, I've redefined what success means to me. A few examples that came to me:

After taking four years of educational classes and submitting an extensive portfolio demonstrating how I applied the knowledge in my work environment, I obtained my CTSM Certification (Certified Trade Show Marketer). The true success in this was that accomplishing it made me more confident in myself professionally, and provided me the courage to speak my opinion.

That same year I obtained certifications from a local college in Illustrator™, Photoshop™ and InDesign™. The true success in this is that I can now use these tools to share my artistic abilities with a bigger audience.

Within seven years of selling the home I co-owned with my ex for a loss to avoid foreclosure, at the age of fifty, I bought my own home for myself and my sons. Rather than living in turmoil and uncertainty as we used to, we now enjoy better, closer relationships in the peaceful home environment I've created. This was no small accomplishment.

And there have been major, life-changing shifts in my knowledge and self-awareness.

Stepping into the River

On the day I was scheduled to attend a work meeting where I would learn the fate of my continued employment, I awoke to this passage in my daily devotional:

As soon as the priests…set foot in the Jordan, its waters…will be cut off (Joshua 3:13).

The Israelites were not to wait in the camp until the Jordan was opened but to "walk by faith" (2 Cor. 5:7 KJV).

They were to break camp, pack up their belongings, form a marching line, and actually step into the river before it would be opened. If they had come down to the riverbank and then stopped, waiting for the water to divide before stepping into it, they would have waited in vain. They were told to "set foot in the Jordan" before "its waters…will be cut off." We must learn to take God at His word and walk straight ahead in obedience, even when we can see no way to go forward. The reason we are so often sidetracked by difficulties is that we expect to see barriers removed before we even try to pass through them. If we would only move straight ahead in faith, the path would be opened for us. But we stand still, waiting for the obstacle to be removed, when we ought to go forward as if there were no obstacles at all. L.B. Cowman

Reading this, I realized that obstacles would not be cleared until I began moving in faith toward my destiny. I walked into the meeting that day knowing that whatever the outcome, this was where my path lay and I was at peace with it.

In the meeting I was informed I would be losing my job. Rather than panicking, as I might have done just a few short years ago, I recognized it as an ideal opportunity to redesign my life.

When I began my career, making money was the primary goal. Now I have a chance to design my life with joy and fulfillment as my main intention.

Incorporating my creative talents into my everyday life has become a priority. I no longer allow my passions to wait in the wings while other, less important things take center stage in my life.

While I do have moments of anxiety about where I will be a year from now and beyond, those moments pale in comparison to the excitement I feel about my future. My focus is fixed on the simpler, more important things in life, like using my talents to benefit and serve others.

I have three sons of whom I'm very proud. More than anything, I want them to be happy. That alone makes me want to continually strive to be a better person and role model. I'm certain the most important thing I can do for my children is for them to see ME happy.

And so, I reflect back on myself as a three-year-old, trapped in an oxygen tank, feeling alone, forgotten and disconnected from everyone. And the arrival of works of art, however simple, created just for me. Reminding me that I'm not alone, I'm not forgotten, that I am connected.

And I know, in a place deep inside of me that can't be touched by hardship or struggle, by layoffs or failed marriages, that this is the reason I've been given these creative gifts. Bringing joy, connection and happiness to others through my artistic ability.

This is me, living my happily ever after.

CJ's Tips on Showing Up *fashionably* LATE for:
Discovering the Source of Your Happiness

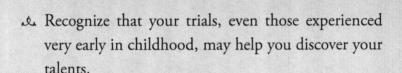

𝒜 Recognize that your trials, even those experienced very early in childhood, may help you discover your talents.

𝒜 Trust your own intuition, more than anything else. Acknowledge when something feels right and true for you.

𝒜 Keep your passions at the center of your life, rather than something you dabble in outside of all your other goals and obligations. If you have a talent that's been sitting on a shelf, take it down and make it a part of your life.

𝒜 Obstacles will not be removed until you start moving toward what you desire. Move forward in faith.

𝒜 Your happily ever after is happening right now. You've only to recognize and cultivate how you're using your gifts to serve others.

Sherri Smith is an certified Cultural Transformation Coach (CT), certified Success Principles Coach, certified Crystal Healer (CCH), and a number one best selling and award winning author. Sherri has a passion and proven ability of understanding others and developing their talent. She helps organizations focus on the right combination of people and performance required to succeed. She also helps people get from where they are to where they want to be. Sheri holds certificates from Cornell University in High Performance Leadership, Change Leadership, and Managing for Execution. She has a master's degree in human resources and management, and a master's certification in elementary education. You can contact Sherri at *sherri@legacybyyourdesign.com*

Chapter Eleven

No Regrets!

by Sherri Smith

*"Of all the words of mice and men, the saddest are,
'It might have been.'"*

Kurt Vonnegut

It had been a tough battle for me, both physically and emotionally, and I wasn't the one who was nearing their last breath. It was my mother, and as I looked into her beautiful dark brown eyes, I saw something different. Not fear of dying or even exhaustion from the fight, strangely enough. This look was different.

Had it always been there? I didn't know for certain. To me, her eyes expressed her soul and the discontent she felt, perhaps like she hadn't really lived the life that she'd wanted.

It wasn't that she was unhappy, really.

Sadly, I could only speculate.

She had always given us, me and my siblings, so much that she hadn't reserved any energy for herself, so she could get what she wanted out of life, too. Had her dreams gone dormant and then dissipated like an evaporating cloud?

I thought back to when I was a little girl. I was so fortunate that my mom was there by me and didn't work at that time. She didn't get a job until I was older. There was this memory that flooded into my mind, perhaps coming back to me at just the right moment for me to learn its valuable lesson.

Mom had asked, "What do you want to be when you grow up, Sherri?"

I'd looked at her and thought for a moment.

For me, the answer was simple. I said, "I want to be a stay-at-home mom, just like you."

Then she told me that she wished more for me than that. At the time, I didn't get it. But I was so young, maybe nine, and I moved on – my curious youthful innocence ready to think about something else.

Finding Me, Being Me

"At the center of your being you have the answer;
you know who you are and you know what you want."

Lao Tzu

As a young adult, I'd spent a great deal of time feeling frustrated by my own discontent, wishing that I would be more "normal," like my parents. In my experience, "normal" meant a steady paycheck, holding the same job long-term, planning for retirement someday. That was so unappealing, although I couldn't specify why. All I knew was that they were steadfastly content and consistent, while I was discontent and definitely inconsistent.

Despite being a teacher and having the wonderful honor of reaching out to children and trying to be a positive light in their young, developing minds, I felt that my internal light was so dim. Something wasn't adding up and I was fearful to evaluate me.

Instead, I chose to focus on everything around me. I thought it would all work out if I could only find a way to make my external environment heal my internal chaos. And I did try…

I moved across the country and entered into the corporate world. It didn't work. Justification set in – I'd just chosen the wrong thing.

Next, I tried my hand at being a children's author. And then a make-up artist. Neither worked out.

And worse – I started to feel like a failure. Why was nothing bringing me fulfillment?

Through everything I tried in order to "find myself," my husband and children remained by me. They were so supportive, and comforted me when things went awry. But I didn't feel better. Finally, my life had the shake-up I'd been seeking, but it was not at all in the way I desired.

I found out that I had cancer.

This discovery not only explained my exhaustion, but it changed my entire life in a single instant.

I had a serious battle ahead of me. I hadn't even figured out what I was meant to do with my life yet, and now it was possible it was coming to an end? Are you kidding me?

Well, I'm not a quitter, so I fought. And I won.

Going through this battle gave me a new opportunity – to be a stay-at-home mom.

The life of a stay-at-home mom is busy – most people acknowledge this to be true. Many women are incredible at it and find fulfillment in it. Initially, I loved it, too. I got to cook more, which I loved. I could be there in "stress-free mode" for my kids. I tried to do it all.

However, the core problem still existed. My external environment, which was what I had always wanted, was not creating a fulfilling or content internal environment.

In fact, something inside of me that I didn't even recognize was screaming at me to pay attention. "Wake up, Sherri! You're no fool; find out what's missing!"

"Life is one big road with lots of signs. So when you're riding through the ruts, don't complicate your mind. Flee from hate, mischief and jealousy. Don't bury your thoughts, put your vision to reality. Wake Up and Live!"

Bob Marley

I looked at my life and how I was living it. I was great at being busy, because it felt productive. This is a trap!

It's when you slow down that things get serious and your mind can get busy.

Signs are everywhere, doing everything they can to gain our attention. But if we don't want to admit what we're lacking, we're only going to keep getting by. That is a regret that is hard to swallow!

One day I was on my Facebook® page and saw a post from an always optimistic and happy friend. She was completely and thoroughly authentic.

The post was about a transformational seminar she had attended, and something in her words made that voice in my head shout, "Do it!"

For the first time, I listened to that voice. That voice that I now know was my intuition.

I walked in to that seminar skeptical, and walked out with a sense of purpose. Okay, at least a direction in which to start…

Going and Growing and Glowing

> *"Purpose is the reason for your journey.*
> *Passion is the fire that lights the way."*
> Author Unknown

The lesson is simple, although we often arrive at it the hard way. In order to go the right direction in life and grow into our full potential, we have to work.

The more we recognize that, the more we glow from within and shine outward.

Today, I consult as a People Strategist, helping individuals identify key factors that will help them find their successes and joys in both their personal and professional lives.

The process is unique to each individual. After all, we are each unique. However, there are some things you can do, starting now, to begin your "no regrets" life.

And I want to share them with you:

ىل Gain 20/20 vision about today's choices, not just yesterday's actions. Learning lessons from the past is wonderful, but placing attention on what you can do today is what's going to take you places. Begin connecting with yourself again, get to know you, and take action to achieve that personal and/or professional satisfaction you seek. You have the answers!

ىل Recognize that a fulfilled you is better for everyone. There is nothing admirable or endearing about giving everyone your best efforts and ignoring your own needs for growth and nurturing. Worse yet, you put yourself at risk of becoming a martyr. Because when you get upset you'll likely point out all that you do for others without getting anything in return. If you help others and not yourself, that is a choice you've made. Expecting a return lessens the joy of giving.

ىل Evaluate what makes you passionate and explore your interests. Remembering what excites us most is strangely tough to do at times. Taking time to do this is a requirement, though, if you're going to really change things around and adopt a "no regrets" lifestyle. Like the old adage says, "Don't put off until tomorrow what you can do today."

ىل Name one thing you can do, starting today, to connect with your purpose. For me, this was finding a way to begin working with people in a different platform than what I'd done up to a certain point. Once I zoned in on the things that made me happy (which are strengths) everything else I needed to do became clearer.

Be grateful and appreciative. Open up your eyes to your world and your universe. Be grateful that you've acknowledged that you want to change some things. Find joy in the people around you and those unexpected moments where something happens to make you smile. Take note of the special things that happen every day – perhaps that hug from your child. We have so much to be grateful for and the energy that gratitude gives us can really take us to amazing places and emotional spaces.

As your life goes on, know that it's never too late to change. Think about this…When you look into your own eyes in the mirror, what do you see? Regret or fulfillment?

The choice is yours.

Sherri's Tips for Showing Up fashionably LATE for:
A Fulfilled Life

- Pay attention to what you can do today, and take small actions toward what you want.

- Honor your own needs and desires as much as those you're serving. Making a martyr out of yourself serves no one.

- Take the time to rediscover what excites you, what brings you joy.

- Get clear on your life purpose by examining your strengths and what makes you happy.

- In a fulfilled life, there is no substitute for the energy of gratitude and appreciation. Take time each day to notice the abundance around you.

Wendy Burruel is a best-selling author, speaker, and coach who helps people understand how things in their life and at work are connected, and how to maximize those connections to achieve a life they love. She helps her clients achieve happier, more connected lives through her books, workshops, speaking events and YouTube™ channel.

Wendy's philosophy is that connection is critical to our success in work and in life, and it is in understanding our humanity that we can be successful and thrive in our work communities. It is Wendy's dream that we all learn to connect more openly, honestly and authentically with one another. Connect with Wendy at *wendy@ wendyburruel.com.*

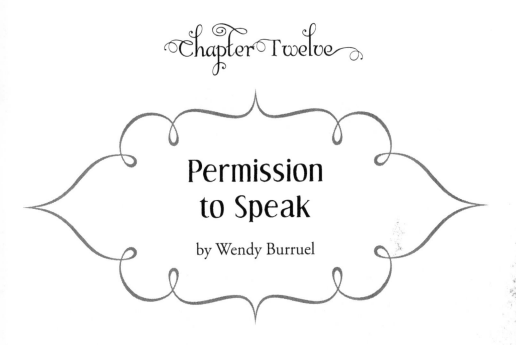

Chapter Twelve

Permission to Speak

by Wendy Burruel

"Don't die with your music still inside of you."

Dr. Wayne Dyer

Have you ever had a moment in your life that was so clearly etched into your brain that you can recall all the details? The sounds, the smells, the way you felt... all of it being so clear in your mind that even though it may have seemed like any ordinary day, something was happening – in your life, in that moment – that was worth remembering? I can remember the day I was first "published" exactly like that.

In my mind, I can still see myself as I reached into the box, pulled out a copy of the book and smiled.

To say it was a "book" is kind of a stretch, but for me, there was magic in it.

When I first held that book in my hands, I remember feeling so proud of the accomplishment at being "published." Sure, it was a photocopied collection of stories from high school students that my English teacher created, but holding it in my hands ignited the desire in me to be a published author.

Even at seventeen years old, I loved to write and wanted to make my voice known to the world. I would spend hours in bookstores combing the stacks of psychology and self-help books, imagining that my book was one of the many on the shelf. It was just so clear in my mind back then.

When I talk about that book now and the fire that was so clearly lit within me at seventeen, you may well wonder why it took me over twenty-five years to become a published author.

Two reasons:

1. Life got in the way.

2. I stopped listening to that voice inside that called out for me to write and share my voice with the world.

At seventeen, I knew that I wanted to be a therapist and a writer. I wanted to help people and I knew I would do this through my writing and through one-on-one therapeutic sessions with people who needed my help.

Pursuing a career as a therapist, I got both a BA and MA in Psychology. I was working for Silicon Valley companies while going to school to help pay for my education. Sometimes working three jobs and going to school at the same time. It was a bit chaotic in my life as a newlywed. After graduate school, it became clear that I could not afford to live in the Bay Area on the wages that I would make as a therapist. I made the tough decision to recommit to working in business by telling myself that I could always switch tracks and come back to being a therapist later in life. This decision would lead me to work for both small and large companies like A&E Television Networks and Yahoo!. And my career took off. Friends got married and had babies. I got divorced.

You know, life happened.

And I stopped listening to the voice inside. I never wrote…not even in journals, for I feared that someone would find them and I would be exposed. I settled into my life and I silenced that voice within that was calling out to write and publish books in order to help others.

Buried Voice

I knew that I was allowing my inner voice to be silenced simply because of life's distractions. What I wasn't consciously aware of was that I was also crippled by a traumatic event in my past.

Until 2014, when it came rushing back into focus.

At a conference for speakers, we were expected to get up and speak in front of the group. Dreading my turn, I had been sick the entire time. By the time I was called upon to speak, I was literally losing my voice.

You know that feeling when you start to say something and only air comes out?

Yeah…exactly that.

It felt like something was stuck in my throat, but it felt bigger than a mere cold. It was like something was energetically and physically restraining my voice.

A clinician who specializes in the connection between the mind and body was at the event, and I was able to do a therapeutic process with her, where I relived this event from my teen years that I hadn't realized was still impacting my life.

You see, I was raped when I was in high school.

A guy that I trusted forced himself on me and covered my mouth with his hand. I couldn't overpower him. I couldn't escape. With his hand over my mouth, I couldn't even scream.

For a variety of reasons, I stuffed that event down and didn't talk about it again for years.

During this therapeutic mind/body session at the speakers' conference, I was encouraged to mentally and emotionally relive the rape, including the awful memory of his hand over my mouth, suppressing my screams. The clinician asked me to scream out loud while visualizing the rape. Yet even with no actual hand over my mouth, I was still unable to scream. I was paralyzed and couldn't seem to force the sound out of my throat.

Then the most powerful thing happened…the scream that had been stifled for over 25 years came roaring out. I screamed loud and long. I cried.

And then, when I had released this primal scream that had been trapped in my body and in my soul, I was able to "re-frame" that event so the memory had a different ending in my brain and in my body.

And it finally dawned on me -- I had been living my life with his hand over my mouth for years.

I had been silencing myself and disconnecting from others. I had been drowning out the voice that was so loud in high school… the voice that wanted to be a published author.

I began to see the key to success as being connected to yourself and not tuning out the voice that is driving you to achieve your life's purpose.

When I was more connected to myself, I found that I had the desire to connect with others around me. Not just friends and family, but also with strangers that I'd meet in my day-to-day adventures. I found myself being more aware of what was going on in my body and in my mind. And as I was more aware of what I needed, it became easier to have more heartfelt, genuine connections with those around me.

I started writing immediately, both journaling and developing content to be published. I had no idea where it would be published, but I was aware that I had opened the floodgates and I was well on my way to publishing something, somehow.

Published Author, At Last

The content that I had been writing became what I published in the book, *The Soul of Success*. It was published in September 2015 and became an International Best-Seller. I wrote about connection and how our lives are more successful and joy-filled when we are connected to ourselves, to each other and to our purpose in life. I was able to share this content with the world because I had tuned into my experiences and was able to see how I was holding myself back and how my history was holding me back (without me being consciously aware of it). It was in connecting to myself that I was able to achieve my dreams and it taught me the importance of connection.

When *The Soul of Success* books arrived at my house, I opened the box, reached in and pulled out a book.

And smiled.

I had finally realized a dream ignited when I was just seventeen. I may have arrived fashionably LATE, but at forty-three, I had finally arrived as a published author!

My life has changed since I published that first book, in that I find that I no longer censor myself. It's as if removing the imaginary hand that was over my mouth for years has given me permission to speak and I'm now freely writing, publishing and sharing content with people to help them. My career didn't take the path that I thought it would, but today I am doing what I wanted to do when I was seventeen…writing and helping people.

A Twenty-Five Year Speed Bump

So, who stopped me from publishing for over twenty-five years when I knew it was a desire that lit up my soul?

ME!

It's easy to articulate the things and people that are obstacles in the way of our success. But profound progress and growth occur when we acknowledge that WE are the one standing in our own way.

In my case, I was holding myself back with the day-to-day life excuses that prevented me from publishing. And I was also held back by trauma that I had buried in my unconscious mind. By tuning in and uncovering what was stopping me, I was able to connect to myself and ultimately realize my dream of being a published author.

Avoid "Snoozing" Your Life Away

If you're like I was, you may be too busy with life to see that you're continually hitting the "snooze" button on your heart's desires.

While "snoozing" today is not a bad thing, it is the repeated hitting of the snooze button on your dreams that prevents them from being realized.

We all have a history of hard stuff. Life is not easy for anyone and we all have our stuff to go through in the course of our lives.

Sometimes it's pretty traumatic stuff.

If there is something in your past that's preventing you from moving forward, seek the help of a trained professional to help get you unstuck. This is the one thing I wish I would have done years ago. Getting to the root of what is silencing you and preventing you from living a life that you love is the most important thing you can do for yourself and those who love you.

Some questions for you to consider:

"What did you dream about when you were a child, and is that dream not yet realized, but still alive in you?"

"What is the ONE THING that you want to make sure to do before you die?" (For me, it was to publish a book.)

"What brings you the most JOY? When was the last time that you did it?"

"Are you living with invisible hands over your mouth? Are you holding back, avoiding saying something to someone (or the world)? If so, what is it you want to say?"

"Did you experience a traumatic event in your past that may be holding you back today? If yes, who can you go to for help processing this event?"

"What baby step can you take TODAY to move you in the direction of your dreams?"

You may be surprised that by just taking a few minutes to jot down some thoughts in your journal in answer to the questions above, you can tune into a part of you that you may have been silencing for years. By tuning into your childhood dreams and what brings you joy, you will find the things that make you come alive. And if you're not doing the things that make you come alive today, make sure that you get a plan in place to do them before you run out of days to "snooze" on the alarm.

At the beginning of this chapter, I shared a quote by Dr. Wayne Dyer, *"Don't die with your music still inside of you,"* and I really take that to heart. I hope you do, too.

I believe that we all have unique talents to share with the world – our music – and I encourage you to share your gifts with others before you leave this Earth. Many of us are waiting for someone to give us permission to live our dreams. If you feel like you need permission from someone else to achieve your life dreams, consider this your permission to speak, to share, to love, to achieve and to make an impact. I know you can do it. ☺

Wendy's Tips for Showing Up *fashionably* LATE for:

Achieving a Life-long Dream or Goal

- ♨ Recognize that your trials, even those experienced very early in childhood, may help you discover your talents.

- ♨ Trust your own intuition, more than anything else. Acknowledge when something feels right and true for you.

- ♨ Keep your passions at the center of your life, rather than something you dabble in outside of all your other goals and obligations. If you have a talent that's been sitting on a shelf, take it down and make it a part of your life.

- ♨ Obstacles will not be removed until you start moving toward what you desire. Move forward in faith.

- ♨ Your happily ever after is happening right now. You've only to recognize and cultivate how you're using your gifts to serve others.

Connie Grant is a Top Real Estate Professional in Lethbridge, Alberta, Canada. She is certified in The Canfield Methodology through Jack Canfield. She has studied energy healing and energy medicine since 2001 with many teachers, including Carolyn Myss and Barbara Brennan. She is currently doing her Initiate in Training with Deborah King.

Her approach with her clients is to study their energy field so she may better understand their focus and intention to help them with their goals. Connie's journey to continue to heal her past has allowed her to meet so many incredible people who share a similar journey, forever making her humble. Connie can be reached at *ConnieGrant.com*.

Chapter Thirteen

Share Your Truth

by Connie Grant

"When you stand and share your story in an empowering way, your story will heal you and your story will heal someone else."

Iyanla Vanzant

Bang! The kitten's tiny body jumped as the bullet slammed into it, killing it instantly. *Bang!* The sound echoed through the cold night air. Another kitten, dead the same way. *Bang! Bang! Bang!*

I watched, paralyzed with fear, as my father, in a terrifying mixture of rage and determination, shot the kittens, one at a time. My cat Punky, whom I loved with all my heart, frantically tried to save her babies. With every shot, I felt a piece of me die.

My mom and sister were screaming and begging my dad to put his gun down, but to no avail. He only stopped firing when the entire litter of kittens lay motionless.

His rage not yet spent, he turned and proclaimed to my mom that she needed to know what it's like to lose a child.

And like that, the cold barrel of his gun pressed against my temple.

My only thought was, I'm going to die tonight.

I heard a voice inside me, a voice I believed was God. "Connie," the voice said, "you have suffered so much. If you want to come home now, I understand." Hot tears streaming down my face, I knew I could end my misery that night. I knew I could surrender and finally be at peace.

My dad pushed the gun harder against my head and shouted at me, "Do you want to die?"

My moment of acceptance and resignation passed quickly. Deep down inside of me, I knew I didn't want to die. Mustering strength from I know not where, I lifted my head, looked directly into his eyes and replied quietly, but vehemently, "No, I want to live."

I braced myself for the expected *"bang"* of the gun and the end of my life.

I'll never know what broke through to him, whether it was my direct gaze into his eyes, or the fierceness of my declaration that I wanted to live, or something else entirely. But in the next moment, he fell to his knees, sobbing, the gun discarded on the ground at his side.

My mom went to him and held him in her arms. My sister and I embraced each other.

It was Christmas Eve. I was eight years old.

~ 1996 ~

I was in a courtroom testifying against my father.

The prosecutor indicated an enlarged photo of our acreage where I grew up, and asked me to point to where I saw my dad sexually assault my sister.

In the months leading up to the trial, through multiple interviews, I maintained that while I caught my dad sexually assaulting my sister several times, he never touched me in that way. I remembered some severe beatings, but never any sexual abuse. After three days in court, my dad was found guilty and sentenced for sexually assaulting my sister.

~ 2001 ~

After thirteen years of marriage, I was legally divorced and had been living on my own for a year, with my two small children. I awoke in the middle of the night to a startling clear memory.

My dad has entered my room and I recognize the look on his face. I know he's going to do something bad to me. I whimper as he forces himself on me. I can hear my mom doing dishes in the other room. I hear her turn on the tap so she doesn't have to hear my cries.

Suddenly, I was flooded with sad childhood memories of sexual abuse.

I truly believe that our soul only gives us what we can handle. I also believe that we don't have to handle these things alone. In that moment, I knew I needed a therapist to help me make sense of these memories. I scheduled an appointment with a professionally trained female therapist. I told her my story and that I was wondering if I was crazy.

Were these flashback memories really true or was my mind playing a sick trick on me? If they were real, why were they surfacing now?

She encouraged me to journal, to write down everything as the memories came back to me. Over the next six months, I created a timeline of my childhood. The memories were very painful, but day by day, I learned to cope.

I took up energy healing at Barbara Brennan School of Healing, and began to heal myself. I surrounded myself with understanding and supportive people.

I saw a homeopath, who became a dear friend of mine and helped me clear energy blocks in my body through homeopathic remedies. I meditated, I attended church, and I spent hours upon hours with my children. Determined to break the cycle of abuse that my family had endured for generations, I showered them with my love.

For five years, I continually focused on my healing journey! I analyzed and dissected my personal history. I was a tough kid and fought a lot in elementary school. I was a high-performing athlete and did well academically in junior and senior high school, which brought me confidence and a wide circle of friends.

In my analysis, I realized that I had never valued sex. It was something I did or had, but I never allowed it to affect me emotionally. I had just felt empty and now I finally understood why.

These memories brought me so many tears. The guilt I felt for how I treated friends and boyfriends was intense. It made me sad to realize how I had been hiding and coping with my pain, and had inadvertently passed some of that pain on to others.

I began reaching out to these past friends, acquaintances and boyfriends. I apologized to some in person. For those I hadn't the strength to face, I wrote, and then burned, apology letters. Each letter I wrote and burned helped to heal and liberate me a little more.

~ 2005 ~

A real turning point came during a past regression therapy session where I went back in time to a very painful scene where my dad was abusing me. Rather than allowing the memory to play out as it actually had, I imagined myself looking in his eyes during that experience and telling him I forgave him. I told him that I understood that he endured a lot of abuse as a child as well and that he was doing only what he understood to do. And it was more than just words that I was saying; I felt the forgiveness to the core of my being.

I came out of that therapy session feeling light and healed. The years of journaling and asking for forgiveness were absolutely essential to my healing, but forgiving my dad for what he did to me…truly and finally set me free.

Amazingly, I could sense that by forgiving my father, I had helped heal him, too. I also believe that on a physical "real time" level he knew it, and felt the change in his heart and body.

Every one of us goes through hardships in life. You may not have experienced a childhood this extreme, or perhaps yours was even more difficult. Perhaps your hardships came later in life, as an adult.

The first thing I offer to you is to recognize and acknowledge and allow your pain. Know that the pain is your compass that will guide you through the steps to heal yourself.

In the beginning, I felt helpless, scared, angry, disgusted, guilty, and shamed. And then mortified by all of these "negative" emotions. As I moved into understanding and embracing what happened to me in my childhood, those feelings dissipated and were replaced with hope, sincerity, caring, honesty, trust, forgiveness, and most importantly, love.

I now believe that the voice inside my eight-year-old mind that dark Christmas Eve was, in fact, me. It was my inner guidance that gave me the strength to choose life.

You may find it hard to believe, but, given the opportunity, I wouldn't change my childhood. My experience of life, good and bad, has made me the person I am today. My experiences have taught me to be more open-minded. I have empathy towards others, because of my own painful memories. Yet the empathy doesn't extend to pity, because I understand that their experience is the very thing that will help them to grow.

Considering my less-than-idyllic childhood, you can imagine how much joy it brings me to hear my kids tell me that they admire me and consider me their role model. I am grateful for my kind and caring husband. I am honored to be a team leader for a top real estate team. Most importantly, I am humbled by the fact that my experience has taught me that love is all that matters. Love for myself and love for others.

It is my hope that, if you're feeling overwhelmed by painful experiences, you will honor yourself. Take small steps to come out and share your truth. One way to start the path to healing would be to write it down in a journal. Day-by-day you will become stronger.

Before you know it, the day will come that you will honor your story and share it with others so they may also heal.

Connie's Tips for Arriving fashionably LATE to:

Sharing Your Story

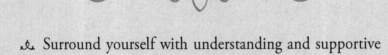

- Surround yourself with understanding and supportive people.

- One of the best ways to heal yourself is to forgive those who have caused you pain.

- Forgiving someone can cause healing to occur in them, even if you don't say it directly to them.

- Journaling is a very effective tool in the healing process.

- Sharing your experience is a way to honor yourself and help others heal at the same time.

Carla White is at her best when she is engaging with people in laughter, entertaining them with her outrageous stories, or empowering them with her witty wisdom.

She is on a mission to encourage people who are fatigued, frustrated, and fed up re-energize and renew their life, through her books, seminars, and retreats.

Carla brings positive energy to her role as a best-selling author, transformational speaker, and *Showing Up* radio show host.

Her greatest creation to date – besides her three beautiful children, of course – is her book, Showing Up: Lessons in Happiness, Humour, and the Courageous Heart.

Chapter Fourteen

Forged
by Fire

by Carla White

"Life doesn't demand perfection. It doesn't require you to be fearless, confident or self-assured. It simply requires that you keep showing up."

Marie Forleo

"That's it. Our house is gone." My husband Stewart calmly gave voice to the inconceivable thoughts swirling through my mind like so much smoke. We were standing by the river, watching a wildfire ravage our city of Fort McMurray, Canada. The surreal scenes that later mesmerized the world on media were a terrifying reality surrounding us in that moment.

The hour before had been frantic. Watching the orange glow of the sky as the fire approached, trying and failing to contact my kids at school, calling Stew home from work, attempting to pack not only the essentials for a family of five, but a lifetime of memories in a few short moments, and then hearing the emergency evacuation alert beacon scream through the radio. Adrenaline was coursing through me like water through a firehose.

We escaped our small subdivision, nestled in the valley, just as the first flames were visible behind our house.

The night was total chaos as thousands of people fled the inferno, jamming the roadways and the single highway that led out of town. Stew saw an opening and took an exit ramp rather than sit in the bumper-to-bumper traffic. I was anxious to make our way to the other side of the city where our three children, Sianna, Rylee, and Shaelyn, had found refuge at an evacuation centre.

As Stew pulled into a parking lot, I began to sob as the first waves of hysteria moved through me. Stew, whose answer to every life challenge is exercise, said,

"Let's get out and you can walk this off."

I complied and started to walk, then stopped to double over. Because, of course, in my muddled thinking, doubling over would somehow make it easier to suck in the air I needed to support my meltdown!

He paused beside me and asked, "Do I have to worry about you? Are you going to be okay?"

In a moment of pure clarity, and perhaps a little bit of defiance, I put my hand up and gasped, "THIS is part of the process! It'll pass; just give me a minute."

I regained my composure (and was able to once again stand upright) just in time to see the forest behind our house engulfed in monstrous flames which then moved rapidly toward the highway where people sat vulnerably in their vehicles. Fear for their safety had my stomach in knots.

Smoke stung our eyes as ash showered us, catching in our throats. Breathing was difficult, though I wasn't sure how much of that was physical and how much was emotional.

Needing to move on, we get back in our vehicle and rejoined the traffic.

Progress was slow, so once again Stew pulled off the road and parked along the riverbank, intent on watching as the hill on the other side of our house burned.

Three minutes.

That's how long it took for the hill to burn from top to bottom, with a final huge plume of black smoke as it destroyed the houses. I stood in disbelief as Stewart again uttered aloud the thought in my head – our home of twenty-four years was gone.

Ever notice how, in a crisis, different people respond differently?

Well, Stew and I were no exception.

My husband, always calm under pressure, picked up his phone, called the insurance company and calmly stated, "I'd like to open a claim for total loss of our home."

I, on the other hand, grabbed my cell phone, shakily dialed my sister's number, and between gulps and gasps for air, finally managed to croak, "It's gone!"

Despite the obvious differences in our respective coping strategies, we held hands in silent comfort as we each concluded our calls.

For my part, I had once again allowed my intense emotion a natural outlet by expressing it, then settled into a sense of quiet calm, and focused on moving forward.

We carried on toward what was most important – our children – who were anxiously awaiting our arrival at the evacuation centre. We arrived just in time to leave again, as the safe haven was now also under threat and further evacuation had been ordered.

Once the kids were with us, I felt surprisingly content. We were together. We were safe. And we were on our way north of the city, away from imminent danger.

It was in those hours, crawling along in the traffic, all of us piled into that vehicle together, that I realized that I'd been given an opportunity. This devastating, tragic, life-changing event was an opportunity for me to choose how I would respond, and how I would show up for myself, for my family, and for my community.

I understood from previous experiences that my greatest lessons, my greatest stages of personal growth, evolved from life's toughest challenges. Resilience was a skill that I had developed over time – through the death of my brother when I was a teenager, my ten-year struggle with depression, and more recently, the tragic death of my fourteen-year-old niece at Christmas.

To me, being resilient is using life experiences to empower and energize us to move forward. These were certainly the most profound emotional challenges I had experienced, healed from and grown through, but they were not the only ones that contributed to how I choose to live my life.

The wildfire was not my first exposure to the fury of Mother Nature! Three years prior, heavy rains had swelled the river behind our house, eroding the banks, and endangering our home, requiring us to be evacuated in the early morning hours. While that situation was far less intense and dangerous than the fire, my response was definitely more dramatic and chaotic!

Picture snot-swinging-sob-fests (plural – as in many of them!) and multitudes of anxious moments fuelled by worry, feeling out of control, fear, and out of proportion hysteria.

In comparison, during the second evacuation there were still plenty of tears and definitely some anxious terrifying moments, but there was a drastic difference in how I felt at my core – aware, peaceful and content – despite the devastation around me.

"Finding serenity in chaos and crisis comes from staying present in the moment, accepting what is rather than what was, and having faith in what the future holds."

Author unknown

That is how I now choose to show up in the world. My blueprint for how to get through anything life throws at me (with a smile) comes down to three simple yet powerful strategies.

Letting Go

Thoughts and beliefs give meaning to our life stories. There is an ongoing dialogue in our head to which we unwittingly pay attention.

For a very long time in my life, that voice (not voices, thank you) was critical, angry, resentful and sad. I was exhausted, carrying all of that baggage around every day.

Part of my healing process was with my feelings – to face them, feel them, deal with them, and heal from them. The realization that I had a choice of whether to interact with these negative thoughts and feelings was extremely liberating.

Once dealt with, I was able to let go and embrace the fun, happier me that had been lost along the way. Admittedly, it is easier to be happy and content when life is moving along nicely, but when Armageddon is unfolding before your very eyes it takes some serious effort!

The wildfire, and subsequent evacuation, was an opportunity for me to test my inner peace and happiness, and this time I flowed through the experience with heightened awareness of my responses. Rather than suppressing as I had done in the past, I acknowledged and allowed each emotion as it came up, expressed it, then easily let it go. This helped me to quickly get to a place of acceptance and a willingness to see this natural disaster in a different way.

Loving

According to the book *A Course In Miracles,* there are only two emotions – love and fear. All other emotions are derived from these two.

Let me be clear, there was plenty to be afraid of in this situation, and it was only once my family was safely evacuated that I could change my perspective away from the distress. In the hours and days after the evacuation, I chose to find evidence of love rather than concentrate on the potentially terrifying images prevalent around me.

And what we focus on, we find.

During the fire and after our departure, what I found was an outpouring of pure acts of love in the form of kindness, generosity, compassion and connection from millions of people around the world. I was lifted and felt secure in the warm embrace of tenderness

Carla White

that was so evident to me, affirming my faith in the humanity and goodness of people. While this event was tragic, it was the love…and laughter that gave me comfort during a challenging time.

Laughing

Laughter helps me increase my energy and improve my mood. Often it is humour in hindsight where I change my perspective to see situations in a ridiculous manner. However, I'm learning to find the funny faster, even during stressful and challenging times.

Referred to as gallows humour, making light of a grim situation is a natural coping strategy for me, and one I use to be more light-hearted. I felt blessed that I was able to maintain my sense of humour throughout our ordeal. Declaring chips a healthy evacuation breakfast, joking about my painfully poor packing job (we somehow ended up with only girls' underwear and nothing for my husband and son), and describing our first night of sleeping in my SUV with my husband and dog – all were stories that kept us and others chuckling.

A Miracle

For thirty hours after our urgent departure, we were convinced that we had watched the devastation of our home.

In fact, we had witnessed a miracle.

Despite the nearly total destruction of the forest and three subdivisions that surround us, our treasured neighbourhood had been spared.

We were evacuees for twenty-nine days and returned gratefully to a damaged but intact home.

As I reflect on our escape from the wildfire – historically, Canada's largest natural disaster and a record-breaking evacuation of 90,000 people – it occurs to me that I have finally shown up as the woman I have always wanted to be.

Living my extraordinary life – laughing, loving and letting go.

Carla's Tips for Showing Up *fashionably* LATE for:

An Extraordinary Life

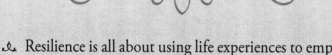

- ♫ Resilience is all about using life experiences to empower and energize us. Consider how your own life challenges have helped you grow, and be grateful for them.

- ♫ Acknowledging and allowing each emotion as it comes up, and expressing rather than suppressing it, makes it so much easier to let it go. Doing this will help you to quickly heal and grow from life's challenges.

- ♫ We find what we focus on. Choose to find evidence of love, rather than fear, and love will surely appear.

- ♫ When faced with stressful situations, stop and ask yourself what is funny about it. Laughter energizes you and improves your mood.

- ♫ In every situation, ask yourself if you're showing up as the woman you always wanted to be. Let your answer guide your next steps, and you'll be living your own extraordinary life!